Economics Re

By the same author

ELEMENTARY ECONOMICS
WORKBOOK FOR ELEMENTARY ECONOMICS
INTERMEDIATE ECONOMICS
MULTIPLE-CHOICE QUESTIONS FOR
INTERMEDIATE ECONOMICS
THE BRITISH CONSTITUTION AND POLITICS
(*with L. Bather*)
HOW BRITAIN IS GOVERNED
WORKBOOK FOR HOW BRITAIN IS GOVERNED
PRODUCING AND SPENDING (*with M. Harvey*)
MODERN ECONOMICS: STUDY GUIDE AND
WORKBOOK (*with M. K. Johnson*)
INTRODUCTION TO MACRO-ECONOMICS
(*with M. K. Johnson*)
INTRODUCTION TO MACRO-ECONOMICS:
A WORKBOOK (*with M. K. Johnson*)
GOVERNMENT AND PEOPLE (*with M. Harvey*)
THE ORGANISATION IN ITS ENVIRONMENT
THE ORGANISATION IN ITS ENVIRONMENT:
ASSIGNMENTS FOR BEC COURSES
(*with J. Chilver*)
BASIC ECONOMICS
WORKBOOK FOR BASIC ECONOMICS
URBAN LAND ECONOMICS
MASTERING ECONOMICS
MODERN ECONOMICS

ECONOMICS REVISION GUIDE

Jack Harvey
B.Sc. (Econ.), Dip. Ed. (Oxford)

© Jack Harvey 1994

All rights reserved. No reproduction, copy or transmission of this publication may be made without written permission.

No paragraph of this publication may be reproduced, copied or transmitted save with written permission or in accordance with the provisions of the Copyright, Designs and Patents Act 1988, or under the terms of any licence permitting limited copying issued by the Copyright Licensing Agency, 90 Tottenham Court Road, London W1P 9HE.

Any person who does any unauthorised act in relation to this publication may be liable to criminal prosecution and civil claims for damages.

First published 1994 by
THE MACMILLAN PRESS LTD
Houndmills, Basingstoke, Hampshire RG21 2XS
and London
Companies and representatives
throughout the world

ISBN 0-333-60195-5

A catalogue record for this book is available
from the British Library.

Printed in Hong Kong

Contents

Preface   xvi

I INTRODUCTION

1 What Economics is About   **1**
    1.1 The Economic Problem   1
    1.2 The Scope of Economics   3
    1.3 Positive Economics   3
    1.4 Normative Economics   4
    1.5 Conclusions   4

2 Methods of Allocating Resources   **5**
    2.1 Functions of an Economic System   5
    2.2 The Market Economy   5
    2.3 The Command Economy   6
    2.4 The Mixed Economy   6
    2.5 Micro- and Macroeconomics   7

II WHAT TO PRODUCE

3 How Price is Formed in the Free Market   **8**
    3.1 Value and Price   8
    3.2 Markets   8

3.3	Forces Determining Price	10
3.4	Demand	10
3.5	Supply	11
3.6	The Determination of Price: Market Clearing	12
3.7	Changes in the Conditions of Demand and Supply	12

4 Applications of Demand and Supply Analysis — 14
4.1	The Functions of Price in the Free Market	14
4.2	Further Applications	15

5 A Further Look at Demand — 16
5.1	Why the Demand Curve Normally Slopes Downwards	16
5.2	Exceptional Demand Curves	18
5.3	Price Elasticity of Demand	18
5.4	Other Elasticities of Demand	20

III HOW TO PRODUCE – THE THEORY OF PRODUCTION

6 The Firm — 21
6.1	The Role of the Firm	21
6.2	The Objectives of the Firm	22
6.3	The Decisions of the Firm	23
6.4	What to Produce	23
6.5	The Legal Form of the Firm and Raising the Necessary Capital	23

7 The Organisation and Scale of Production — 27
7.1	The Division of Labour	27
7.2	The Advantages of Large-scale Production	28

	7.3	The Size of Firms	29
	7.4	The Predominance of the Small Firm	29
8	**The Distribution of Goods to the Consumer**		**31**
	8.1	The Scope of Production	31
	8.2	The Wholesaler	31
	8.3	The Retailer	32
	8.4	The Future of the Middleman	33
9	**The Location of Production**		**35**
	9.1	The Advantages of Different Localities	35
	9.2	The Level of Rents in Different Areas	35
	9.3	Conclusions	35
10	**Combining the Factors of Production**		**37**
	10.1	The Law of Diminishing Returns	37
	10.2	The Optimum Combination of Variable Factors	38
11	**Deciding on the Most Profitable Output**		**39**
	11.1	The Costs of Production	39
	11.2	How Do Costs Behave as Output Expands?	40
	11.3	Perfect Competition	41
	11.4	The Short-period Equilibrium Output of the Firm under Perfect Competition	41
	11.5	The Long-period Equilibrium of the Firm and Industry	42
12	**The Supply Curve of the Industry Under Perfect Competition**		**45**
	12.1	Introduction	45
	12.2	The Short Period	45

	12.3	The Long Period	45
	12.4	Elasticity of Supply	46
13	**Rewarding the Factors of Production: the Marginal Productivity Theory of Distribution**		**48**
	13.1	Introduction	48
	13.2	The Marginal Productivity Theory: Perfect Competition	48
	13.3	The Determination of the Price of a Factor Service	49
	13.4	Weaknesses of the Marginal Productivity Theory	50

IV THE GOVERNMENT AND THE ALLOCATION OF RESOURCES

14	**Market Failure and the Role of Government**		**51**
	14.1	Efficiency in the Allocation of Resources	51
	14.2	How Does Market Failure Arise?	52
	14.3	The Economic Functions of Goverment: a Summary	53
	14.4	The Value of 'Perfect Competition' Analysis	53
15	**Monopoly**		**54**
	15.1	Imperfect Competition	54
	15.2	What Do We Mean by 'Monopoly'?	55
	15.3	Foundations of Monopoly Power	55
	15.4	The Equilibrium Output of the Monopolist	56
	15.5	Public Policy and Monopoly	57
	15.6	Discriminating Monopoly	59

16 Imperfect Competition: Other Forms — 60
16.1 Monopolistic Competition — 60
16.2 Oligopoly — 61
16.3 Pricing Policy in the Real World — 61

17 Externalities and Cost-benefit Analysis — 62
17.1 Externalities — 62
17.2 Methods of Dealing with Externalities — 62
17.3 Cost–benefit Analysis: Reasons for — 63
17.4 Difficulties of CBA — 63
17.5 Assessment of the Role of CBA — 64

18 The Environment: Conservation and Pollution — 65
18.1 The Environment as an Economic Good — 65
18.2 Conservation — 65
18.3 Maintaining the Stock of a Renewable Resource: Fish — 66
18.4 Preserving a Non-renewable Resource: an Historic Building — 66
18.5 Pollution — 68

19 The Provision of Goods and Services by the Public Sector — 71
19.1 The Case for Public Sector Provision — 71
19.2 Accountability v. Economic Efficiency — 72
19.3 The Problem of Assessing 'Needs' — 72
19.4 Pricing Policy — 72
19.5 The Nationalised Industries and Privatisation — 73

V REWARDS TO THE DIFFERENT FACTORS OF PRODUCTION

20 Labour and Wages — 76
- 20.1 The Nature of the Labour Force — 76
- 20.2 Methods of Rewarding Labour — 77
- 20.3 The Determination of the Wage Rate in a Particular Industry, Occupation or Locality — 78
- 20.4 Trade Unions: the Process of Collective Bargaining — 80
- 20.5 The Government and Wages — 82

21 Capital and Interest — 83
- 21.1 Capital — 83
- 21.2 Interest — 84

22 Land and Rent — 85
- 22.1 'Land' and 'Rent' as General Terms — 85
- 22.2 Economic Rent – Land and Rent to the Economist — 85

23 Entrepreneurship and Profit — 87
- 23.1 Entrepreneurship — 87
- 23.2 Profit — 87
- 23.3 The Role of Profit in a Market Economy — 88

VI MONEY AND FINANCIAL INSTITUTIONS

24 Money and the Rate of Interest — 89
- 24.1 The Functions of Money — 89
- 24.2 The Demand for Money — 90
- 24.3 The Supply of Money — 91
- 24.4 The Rate of Interest — 92

25 Financial Markets — 95
- 25.1 The Provision of Liquid Capital — 95
- 25.2 Money Markets — 95
- 25.3 The Capital Market — 96
- 25.4 The Stock Exchange — 97

26 Clearing Banks — 98
- 26.1 Types of Banks in the UK — 98
- 26.2 The Creation of Credit — 98
- 26.3 Bank Lending — 99
- 26.4 Modification of the Cash Ratio Approach — 99
- 26.5 The Effects of Recent Increased Competition — 100

27 The Bank of England — 101
- 27.1 Functions of the Bank of England — 101
- 27.2 Principles of Monetary Control — 102
- 27.3 Monetary Base Control — 102
- 27.4 Rate of Interest Control: the Present System — 103

VII THE GOVERNMENT AND STABILISATION POLICY

28 Measuring the Level of Activity: National Income Calculations — 105
- 28.1 The Principle of National Income Calculations — 105
- 28.2 National Income Calculations in Practice — 106
- 28.3 Uses of National Income Statistics — 107
- 28.4 Factors Determining a Country's Material Standard of Living — 108

29 Unemployment — 110
- 29.1 The Nature of Unemployment — 110
- 29.2 The Causes of Unemployment — 111

30 The Level of Output and Aggregate Demand: the Keynesian Explanation — 112
- 30.1 The Link Between Spending and Production — 112
- 30.2 Reasons for Changes in Aggregate Demand — 113
- 30.3 Consumption Spending — 114
- 30.4 Investment Spending — 116
- 30.5 Equilibrium Through Changes in the Level of Income — 119
- 30.6 The Effect of Changes in Consumption — 119
- 30.7 Government Spending and Taxation — 120
- 30.8 The Effect of Foreign Trade — 122
- 30.9 Demand Management — 122

31 Employment and the Price Level — 125
- 31.1 Changes in the Approach to Full Employment — 125
- 31.2 Aggregate Demand and Aggregate Supply — 125
- 31.3 Full Employment and Demand Management — 127
- 31.4 How the Government Can Manage AD — 127
- 31.5 Supply-side Economics — 128
- 31.6 Postscript — 130

32 Inflation: Its Effects — 131
- 32.1 Why Control Inflation? — 131
- 32.2 A Note on Measuring Changes in the General Level of Prices — 133

Contents **xiii**

33	**Policies to Achieve Price Stability**	**134**
	33.1 Causes of Inflation: a Simplified Statement	134
	33.2 Monetarism	136
	33.3 Policy Implications of Monetarist Theory	138
	33.4 Concluding Observations	138
34	**Economic Growth**	**139**
	34.1 The Nature of Growth	139
	34.2 Achieving Growth	139
	34.3 The Government and Growth	140
35	**Balanced Regional Development**	**141**
	35.1 The Regional Problem	141
	35.2 Government Policy	142
	35.3 Inner City Regeneration	144
	35.4 Regional Policy in the Context of the EC	144
	35.5 Appraisal of Regional Policy	145
36	**Public Finance**	**146**
	36.1 The Distribution of Income	146
	36.2 Government Expenditure	146
	36.3 The Modern Approach to Taxation	147
	36.4 The Structure of Taxation	148
	36.5 The Advantages and Disadvantages of Direct Taxes	149
	36.6 The Advantages and Disadvantages of Indirect Taxes	150
	36.7 The Incidence of Taxation	151

VIII INTERNATIONAL TRADE

37	**The Nature of International Trade**	**152**
	37.1 Why International Trade?	152

	37.2 The Advantages of International Trade	153
	37.3 The Terms of Trade	153
	37.4 Free Trade and Protection	154
38	**The Balance of Payments**	**157**
	38.1 Paying for Imports	157
	38.2 The Balance of Payments	157
39	**Foreign Exchange Rates**	**159**
40	**The Correction of a Balance of Payments Disequilibrium**	**161**
	40.1 Alternative Approaches	161
	40.2 Reducing Expenditure on Imports: Deflation	161
	40.3 Expenditure Switching: Depreciation of the Exchange Rate	163
	40.4 Managed Flexibility	164
	40.5 International Liquidity	165
41	**The European Community**	**167**
	41.1 Background to the EC	167
	41.2 Institutions of the EC	168
	41.3 Economic Objectives of the EC	169
	41.4 Advantages for the UK of Belonging to the EC	169
	41.5 Problems Facing the UK as a Member of the EC	170
	41.6 The Single Market: 1993	170

IX LOOKING INTO THE FUTURE

42	**The Population of the UK**	**171**
	42.1 The Growth of Population	171

42.2	Implications of Changes in the Size of the Population	172
42.3	Age Distribution of the Population	173
42.4	The Industrial Distribution of the Working Population	173
42.5	The Geographical Distribution of the Population	174

43 Current Problems and Policies of the UK — 176

43.1	Introduction	176
43.2	Inflation	176
43.3	The UK's Relationship with the EC	178
43.4	Balance of Payments Difficulties	178
43.5	Unemployment	179
43.6	Recent Developments	180

Preface

Many students, especially those studying part-time, have asked for a set of revision notes which will: (*a*) furnish in a 'nutshell' the ground covered by basic economic theory; (*b*) save time in summarising reading; (*c*) indicate interrelationships between the different topics; and (*d*) provide the essentials for pre-examination revision. This book should not be used as a 'crammer', but simply as a supplement to the conscientious study of a main text. While it follows closely Jack Harvey, *Modern Economics*, 6th edn (Macmillan), the subject matter is common to similar books.

The format has been chosen to make it possible to slip the book into an inside jacket pocket or handbag, making it more readily available for reading in the odd moments which might otherwise be wasted. Only essential diagrams are included, but the presentation with subheads and so on is designed to promote learning through a visual impact.

JACK HARVEY

Part I

Introduction

1 What Economics is About

1.1 The Economic Problem

Wants and Limited Means

The economic problem arises because, in comparison with our unlimited wants, we have only limited means. We solve by 'economising' – arranging our expenditure so as to obtain the maximum satisfaction from what resources we do have. The economic problem applies to individual consumers, producers and the government.

Opportunity Cost

Since our means are limited, choosing one good instead of another involves sacrifice. *The best alternative which has to*

2 Introduction

be given up can be regarded as the real or *opportunity cost* of the good which is obtained.

'Free' and 'Scarce' Goods

'Free' goods are those which are so plentiful relative to demand that nobody will give anything for them. *Economic goods* (which includes services) are 'scarce' goods, since they can only be obtained by *giving something else in exchange*.

Production Possibility Curve (PPC)

Figure 1.1 shows the various combinations of goods (simplified to two) obtainable from available resources when fully employed. More intensive use of resources in one line leads to diminishing returns and thus a PPC which is

FIGURE 1.1
A Production-possibility Curve

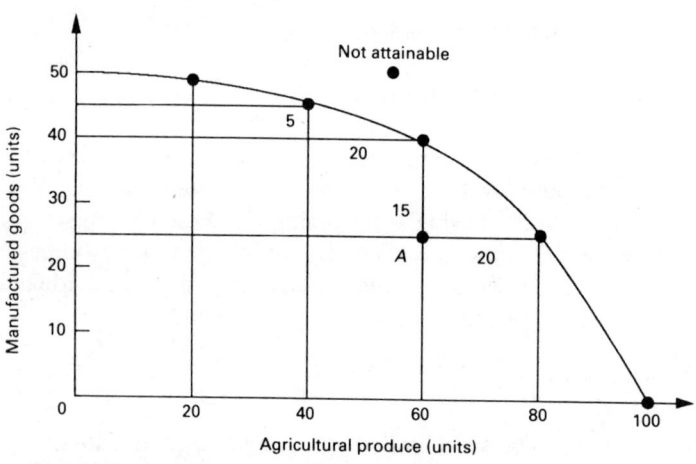

concave to the origin. Points to the north-east of the curve are unattainable.

1.2 The Scope of Economics

Definition: economics is the study of how people allocate their limited resources to provide for their wants.
This means that:

1. Economics is a *social science*.
2. Economics is closely concerned with the findings of *other sciences*.
3. Economics selects a *particular aspect* of human behaviour – where an economic problem exists because: (*a*) ends are unlimited *and* of varying importance; (*b*) means are limited *and* can be used in alternative ways.
4. Economics *accepts ends* as given without judging their merit, though full social costs and benefits must be allowed for.
5. Economics considers how goods are *distributed* between different people.

Difficulties

The economist faces difficulties of: (*a*) carrying out *experiments*; (*b*) *measuring* welfare.

Positive and Normative Economics

Economists proceed as scientifically as possible, but there is some dispute as to how vigorously scientific methods should be applied.

1.3 Positive Economics

This (1) deals only with *objective statements* – those which can be tested by facts; (2) uses *scientific methods* to establish general principles by: (*a*) *induction*: examining facts for causal relationships; or (*b*) *deduction*: from given assumptions deriving propositions by logical reasoning (often described as 'model-building'). Sequence is: (*i*) selection of problem; (*ii*) assumptions; (*iii*) hypothesis by logical reasoning from assumptions; (*iv*) test hypothesis; (*v*) if not refuted, use hypothesis for prediction.

1.4 Normative Economics

This follows the scientific prediction technique of positive economics, but uses it to suggest what action should be taken to achieve given *policy objectives*.

1.5 Conclusions

Why Economists Disagree

Although propositions may have been obtained scientifically, *economists can disagree* because:

1. Facts are deficient.
2. Doubts on causal connection between facts afford alternative explanations.
3. Some propositions contain hidden value judgments.
4. Unconscious individual bias may affect analysis.

The Economist as a Consultant

In a *business enterprise*, the objective of the economist is to enhance profits. With *government policy*, the final decision is political, but the economist can: (*a*) expose any inconsistency between aims; (*b*) indicate the full implications of a particular policy; (*c*) recommend more economic ways of achieving a given end.

2 Methods of Allocating Resources

2.1 Functions of an Economic System

The Role of the Economic System

We economise by: (*a*) arranging wants in order and satisfying the most important first; (*b*) using factors of production as efficiently as possible. Thus any economic system must answer: *What? How much? How? For whom?* In doing so it links *firms* and *households*.

There are two broad systems: (*a*) the market economy, working through the free price system; (*b*) the command economy.

2.2 The Market Economy

Here the price system indicates the goods wanted by consumers and allocates the community's resources to produce those goods through the profit motive. Earnings of the factors of production decide how those goods shall be distributed.

Although the price system overcomes many of the difficulties of the command economy, it has *defects:*

1. It cannot provide for *'community goods'* which are not marketable because free-riders cannot be excluded (see Chap. 19).
2. Competition may not occur in practice because of *monopoly powers*.
3. *Imperfect knowledge or immobilities* may prevent an easy adjustment of supply to price changes.
4. It ignores *social costs* and *social benefits*.
5. Some forms of competition, e.g. competitive advertising, lead to *inefficient* use of resources.
6. *Consumers' choice may be distorted* by persuasive advertising.
7. Instability of the economy can lead to *unemployment* and *inadequate growth*.
8. It accepts, and even accentuates, *inequalities of income*.

2.3 The Command Economy

Merits correspond closely to the defects of the market economy. In particular, it estimates wants, directs resources, accordingly, and distributes the goods produced. But it faces difficulties of:

1. Estimating wants.
2. Operating through a bureaucracy.
3. Co-ordination.
4. Reducing private incentives.
5. Restricting individual freedom.

2.4 The Mixed Economy

We need not discard the advantages of the private enterprise system. Britain has a mixed economy, about one quarter of total production being undertaken by the public sector (government, local authorities and nationalised industries). But even in the remaining private sector, the government intervenes to varying degrees in order to deal with the different forms of market failure.

2.5 Micro- and Macroeconomics

Microeconomics: studies how goods and productive services are allocated and rewarded by the market mechanism, and how their prices are interrelated.

Macroeconomics: studies the overall level of activity and the general level of prices by looking at *aggregate* demand and *aggregate* supply flows.

Part II

What to Produce

3 How Price is Formed in the Free Market

3.1 Value and Price

The value of a good is the rate at which it exchanges for other goods. This rate is usually expressed in money terms as a *price*. Thus, by comparing prices, we can compare the rates at which different goods can be exchanged.

Changes in relative prices are the signals which indicate changes in demand or changes in the conditions upon which goods can be produced. These signals are flashed up in the market.

3.2 Markets

Definition: a market consists of all those buyers and sellers of a good who influence its price.

World Markets

A commodity has a world market if a change in its price in one part of the world affects its price in the rest of the world. For a commodity to have a world market, it must: (*a*) have a wide demand; (*b*) be transportable; (*c*) have low transport costs relative to its value; (*d*) be durable.

Perfect and Imperfect Markets

Where differences in the price of a good in different parts of the market are eliminated quickly, there is a *perfect* market. For this to be the case, buyers and sellers must: (*a*) have exact *knowledge* of the prices being paid in different parts of the market: (*b*) base their actions solely on *price*. Professional dealers in a commodity make for a perfect market.

In contrast, retail markets tend to be *imperfect*. Here price differences persist because sellers and, particularly, buyers lack knowledge of market conditions. *Persuasive advertising* makes for an imperfect market, but *informative advertising* helps to make it more perfect.

Organised Produce Markets

These have developed where commodities have a wide market and are in constant demand. Most are still held in recognised buildings. They:

1. Enable manufacturers and wholesalers to obtain *supplies* of a commodity easily, quickly and at the ruling market price.
2. Allow manufacturers to *hedge* against a future rise in the price of their raw materials. For 'futures' dealings, commodities should be (*a*) durable, (*b*) easily graded, (*c*) dealt in often enough to employ professional

dealers, (d) subject to price fluctuations. If a dealer is *optimistic*, he is termed a '*bull*'; if *pessimistic*, a '*bear*'.
3. Even out price fluctuations by dealers holding *stocks*, though speculation may accentuate price changes.

3.3 Forces Determining Price

Price is determined by the interaction of demand and supply. The analysis of the way demand and supply work in the egg market is simplified by assuming: (a) a single grade of egg; (b) no transport costs within the market; (c) many small competitive buyers and sellers; (d) a perfect market; (e) no government interference in the free operation of market forces.

3.4 Demand

Definition: demand is how much of a good persons would be willing and able to buy at a given price over a given period of time. Demand is determined by: (a) price; (b) the conditions of demand (Fig. 3.1).

1. Price, the Conditions of Demand Remaining Unchanged

Normally more will be demanded the lower the price. How much would be demanded at different prices in the market can be shown in a *demand schedule*.

2. The Conditions of Demand

Demand at any given price may change because of a change in:

(a) the *prices of other goods*, particularly those which are substitutes or complements;

FIGURE 3.1
The Difference between a Change in Demand Resulting from a Lower Price and a Change in the Conditions of Demand

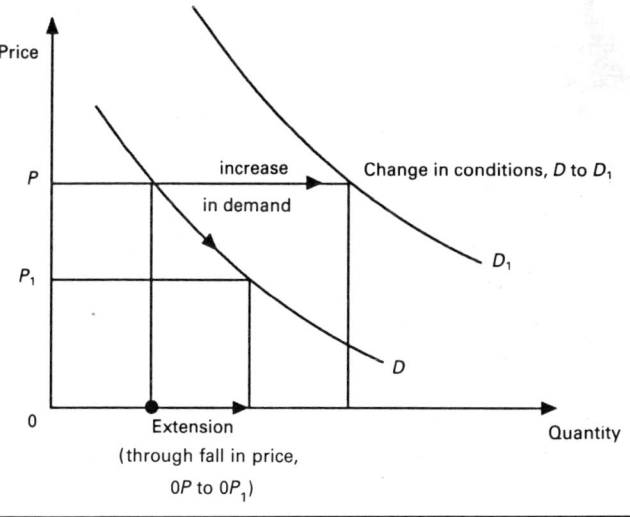

(b) *tastes*;
(c) *expectations* of future price changes;
(d) *government policy*;
(e) *real income*;
(f) the distribution of *wealth*;
(g) the size and composition of the *population*.

3.5 Supply

Definition: supply is how much of a good is offered for sale at a given price over a given period of time. The quantity depends on: (1) price; (2) conditions of supply.

1. Price, the Conditions of Supply Remaining Unchanged

Normally more of a good will be supplied the higher its price. How much would be supplied at different prices in the market can be shown in a *supply schedule*.

Unlike demand, supply takes time to adjust to a price change. Thus different periods of time produce different supply schedules.

2. The Conditions of Supply

Supply at any given price may change because of a change in:

(*a*) *price expectations*;
(*b*) the prices of *other goods*;
(*c*) the prices of *factors* of production;
(*d*) *natural* conditions or *abnormal* circumstances;
(*e*) *government* policy;
(*f*) *techniques*;
(*g*) *sources* of supply of raw materials;
(*h*) *new firms* entering the industry.

3.6 The Determination of Price: Market Clearing

The *equilibrium or market price* is that where the quantity demanded is equal to the quantity which sellers are willing to supply. It is the price where demand and supply curves cut. At any price below the market price, demand exceeds supply; at any price above, supply exceeds demand.

3.7 Changes in the Conditions of Demand and Supply

A change in the conditions of demand will lead to a new equilibrium price. Assuming that the conditions of supply do not alter, an increase in demand will produce a rise in price; a decrease, a fall.

Similarly, assuming conditions of demand do not change, an increase in supply will produce a fall in price; a decrease, a rise.

4 Applications of Demand and Supply Analysis

4.1 The Functions of Price in the Free Market

Price allocates, indicates, motivates and distributes.

1. *It 'rations out' scarce goods.* Price can be used to decide, for example, who obtains: (*a*) scarce parking space; (*b*) scarce Cup Final tickets – where the 'spiv' price allocates.
2. *It indicates changes in wants.* An increase in demand, e.g. for housing, is signalled by a rise in price.
3. *It induces supply to respond to changes in demand.* When demand increases, price rises and supply expands.
4. *It indicates changes in the conditions upon which goods can be supplied.* If the cost of producing a good rises (e.g. because raw materials cost more) it is signalled by a price rise. Consumers can pay this higher price or switch to other goods.
5. *It rewards the factors of production.* When the price of a good rises, producers can offer higher rewards to attract factors in order to expand output. These factors, therefore, obtain a larger share of the 'cake' produced.

4.2 Further Applications

1. *Prices of agricultural products fluctuate* more than the prices of manufactured goods because the conditions of supply of agricultural products change more frequently than those of manufactured goods.
2. *An increase in the demand for cars causes the price of tyres to rise* (complements, joint demand).
3. *An increase in the demand for petrol leads to a rise in its price but a fall in the price of paraffin* (joint supply).
4. *The government can increase demand for a good*, e.g. coal, by a *subsidy*, especially if a tax is levied on substitutes, e.g. oil. Alternatively, it could try to influence demand by *advertising* the advantages of coal.

5 A Further Look at Demand

5.1 Why the Demand Curve Normally Slopes Downwards

Maximising Satisfaction

An individual who acts rationally will seek to obtain the maximum total satisfaction from limited resources. To do this, he balances the opportunity cost of various goods against the satisfaction each gives him. Usually the choice takes the form of a bit more of one good against a little bit less of another.

Preliminary Assumptions

(*a*) A housewife; (*b*) a limited housekeeping allowance; (*c*) she seeks to maximise satisfaction from this allowance; (*d*) income and tastes do not change; (*e*) she knows the satisfaction which each good will give; (*f*) demand is too small to influence price.

1. The Equilibrium Condition

Our housewife will be in equilibrium when she would not switch one penny of expenditure on one good to spending on another.

Utility is the power to satisfy a want. The housewife's

objective is to maximise total utility from her resources. To do this, she considers her spending at the margin: the last *penny* spend on good *A* must afford the same utility as the last *penny* spent on good *B*. Thus *the equilibrium condition* is: the marginal utility of a penny spent on *A* = the marginal utility of a penny spend on *B*.

To allow for some goods being 'lumpy', we have to weight the utility from the last *unit* of a good by its price. Thus:

$$\frac{\text{marginal utility of a unit of } A}{\text{price of unit of } A} = \frac{\text{marginal utility of a unit of } B}{\text{price of unit of } B}$$

2. How Can the Consumer Achieve Equilibrium?

The *law of diminishing marginal utility*: the utility derived from a given addition to a consumer's stock of a good will eventually decline (tastes and the consumption of other goods remaining unchanged). Thus the housewife can arrange that equal utility is derived from the last penny spent on each good by varying the quantities bought.

3. What Happens When Price Changes?

A fall in the price of good *A*, for example, would disturb the equilibrium position:

(*a*) More of good *A* can now be obtained per penny, including the marginal penny. Thus the utility obtained from the last penny has risen. The housewife therefore buys more of *A* to reduce the utility of the last pennyworth.

(*b*) The $\dfrac{MU_A}{P_A} = \dfrac{MU_B}{P_B}$ relationship is destroyed when the price of *A* falls. To restore the equality, the marginal utility of *A* must be lowered – by buying more *A*.

18 What to Produce

By both approaches, therefore, more is demanded when price falls. This applies also to the market, the aggregate of the demand of the individual buyers.

5.2 Exceptional Demand Curves

There are three main cases where *less* of a good may be demanded as its price falls:

1. *Inferior goods.* A fall in the price of a good on which a large part of income is spent will increase real income. This allows superior goods to be bought, which could replace inferior goods.
2. *Expectations* of further price changes in the same direction.
3. *'Snob appeal'* goods are not wanted when many can afford them, though this is more likely for individual demand than market demand.

5.3 Price Elasticity of Demand (*e of d*)

Measurement

The degree to which demand responds to a change in price is measured by the *elasticity of demand*. This compares the *rate* at which demand changes with the *rate* of the price change bringing it about.

1. Elasticity of demand $= \dfrac{\text{proportionate change in demand}}{\text{proportionate change in price}}$

$$= \dfrac{\dfrac{\Delta Q}{Q}}{\dfrac{\Delta P}{P}} = \dfrac{\dfrac{\text{new } Q - \text{old } Q}{\text{old } Q}}{\dfrac{\text{new } P - \text{old } P}{\text{old } P}}$$

If *e of d* is greater than 1, demand is elastic.
If *e of d* is less than 1, demand is inelastic.
If *e of d* equals 1, elasticity equals unity.
2. If price falls, and total outlay increases, demand is elastic. If price rises, and total outlay increases, demand is inelastic, and vice versa.

Rule: demand is *elastic* if total outlay changes in *opposite* direction to the price change; demand is *inelastic* if total outlay changes in *same* direction as the price change.

Points Regarding Elasticity of Demand

1. Demand curves are unlikely to have the same elasticity throughout their length.
2. Important exceptions to 1 are: (*a*) demand absolutely inelastic; (*b*) demand perfectly elastic; (*c*) *e of d* = 1.
3. A straight-line demand curve has a different *e of d* for each price because *rates* depend upon the price and quantity from which we start.
4. Usually we cannot compare the elasticities of demand of different goods by comparing the slopes of their different demand curves because: (*a*) the scales on the graph may differ; (*b*) see (3) above.

Factors Determining Elasticity of Demand

1. Availability of *substitutes*.
2. Number of possible *substitute uses*.
3. *Proportion of income* spend on good.
4. Period of *time*.
5. For market demand curve, the possibility of *new purchasers*.

Uses of the Concept

1. *Theoretical economics*: (*a*) to define 'perfect competition'; (*b*) to analyse the effect of changes in the conditions of supply.
2. *Business decisions*: (*a*) supermarket depends upon a high *e of d*; (*b*) monopolist's decisions.
3. *Government policy*: for example, with regard to commodity taxing; the effect of a tax or subsidy on the size of an industry; the incidence of a selective indirect tax; exchange devaluation or depreciation; the effect of changes in the terms of trade on the balance of payments.

5.4 Other Elasticities of Demand

Income elasticity of demand is the proportionate change in demand divided by the proportionate change in real income.

Cross-elasticity of demand is the proportionate change in demand for good X in response to the proportionate change in the price of good Y. For substitutes, cross-elasticity of demand is positive; for complements, it is negative.

Part III

How to Produce – the Theory of Production

6 The Firm

6.1 The Role of the Firm

Definition

Firms are the units which buy and hire productive resources in order to produce goods and services.

The Factors of Production

The classical economists' classification based on physical characteristics – land, labour, capital and organisation – has weaknesses, e.g. compartments overlap. But modern economists still use the classification to distinguish special characteristics useful for analysis:

Land: the resources provided by nature. The concept has been extended to all factors fixed in supply and whose earnings are termed 'economic rent'.

Labour: the effort made by *human* beings in production. The human factor gives rise to problems of mobility, unemployment and psychological attitudes.

Capital: (*a*) *stocks of consumer goods* not yet in the hands of the consumer; and (*b*) *all producer goods*. Producer goods are not wanted for their own sake, but to produce consumer goods. Capital gives rise to problems of sacrificing present consumption and of fluctuations in economic activity.

Enterprise: accepting the risks of producing for an uncertain future. The reward is profit or loss.

Production

Because this consists of satisfying wants (producing utility), it covers services as well as goods, including storing and moving goods.

6.2 The Objectives of the Firm

Firms may have *other objectives* than *maximising profits*:

1. *Personal priorities*, e.g. good labour relations, welfare, power.
2. Managers give priority to their own security or prestige by *maximising sales* or *growth*.
3. *Long-term advantages*.
4. *Public image* (monopolies).
5. Deference to *government guidelines*.

But profits have to be made to stay in business. Thus *we assume that firms seek to maximise profits*.

6.3 The Decisions of the Firm

The firm has to decide on:

1. What to produce.
2. Its legal form and raising capital.
3. Techniques and scale of operations.
4. Location.
5. Product distribution.
6. Combination of resources.
7. Size of output.
8. Labour relations.

6.4 What to Produce

A firm looks to *return on capital*. Deciding what good(s) to produce will probably rest on: (*a*) first-hand knowledge; (*b*) research, through own desk research, commissioned market research, test marketing.

6.5 The Legal Form of the Firm and Raising the Necessary Capital

The firm's legal form is often linked with *raising capital*.

Working capital, for purchasing single-use factors, can be obtained from banks, trade credit, advance deposits, hire-purchase companies, factor houses, tax reserves, inter-company finance, advance deposits and the government.

Fixed capital, for purchasing factors used many times, is more difficult to raise, especially for the small firm.

Sole Proprietor

Here ownership is vested in one person, whatever the size

of business. The *advantages* are: (*a*) personal control; (*b*) personal rewards for energy and initiative. But there are *disadvantages*: (*a*) *sources of capital limited* to personal savings, borrowing from friends and profits ploughed back; (*b*) no limited liability: (*c*) discontinuity.

Partnership

Normally two to twenty persons who can bring extra capital and specialised skills into the business. *Disadvantages*: (*a*) similar to those of small proprietor; (*b*) each partner responsible for action of others, *increasing* the *risk* of unlimited liability.

Joint-stock Company

Advantages: (*a*) *limited liability* (first bestowed in 1855); (*b*) *continuity*; (*c*) availability of *capital*. *Disadvantages*: (*a*) *capital gains tax* is paid on assets sold by the company and again on shares which have increased in value when sold; (*b*) possible *loss of controlling interest*.

The *finance* of a company is obtained by: (*a*) selling *shares*; (*b*) borrowing through *debentures*; (*c*) government grants or loans (*d*) retaining profits. The *differences* between shares and debentures are:

	(*a*) *Ordinary share*	(*b*) *Debenture*
Definition	a share in the company, accepting risks	loan
Redemption date	no	yes
Yield to investor	based on profits	fixed rate of interest
Voting rights	yes, per share	none, if interest paid

Priority of repayment	last claim	prior claim
Power to enforce liquidation	nil	if interest not paid
Hedge against inflation	profits rise	no, fixed money yield

A company is said to be *highly geared* if the value of fixed interest loans is high compared with share capital. High-gearing has *advantages*: (*a*) if *profits* are good; (*b*) interest on debentures is a cost for *tax* purposes.

Government grants and loans are available in Development Areas (see Chap. 35) and to farmers for certain improvements.

Retained profits are the major source of capital for expansion.

Private and Public Companies

The *private company* is one which is not a public company and has no more than fifty shareholders. It has *limited liability*, but can still be privately owned and managed. It can raise capital by: (*a*) ploughing back profits; (*b*) a 'private placing' of shares; (*c*) tapping special government sources; (*d*) borrowing from banks, merchant banks and specialised finance corporations, e.g. 3i.

The *public company* must have at least two shareholders, a minimum authorised capital of £50 000 and be designated 'Plc'. Raising capital really involves shares being quoted on the Stock Exchange. Capital can then be obtained by: (*a*) a *Stock Exchange 'placing'* (for less than about £15 mn.); (*b*) an *offer for sale* (up to £50 mn.); (*c*) a *public issue by prospectus* (over £50 mn.), where an *issuing house* arranges *underwriting*, and shares are bought by '*stags*' as well as by the public; (*d*) a '*rights*' issue to existing shareholders.

Co-operative Societies

These account for 5 per cent of Britain's retail trade. They are owned by members who hold £1 shares, but a person has only one vote irrespective of the number of shares held. Profits are distributed according to purchases, but redeemable stamps have tended to replace the 'divi'.

Some *producers*' co-operatives now exist in agriculture, replacing the old Marketing Boards.

The Public Sector

Production in the public sector may be by government department, public corporation, quasi-government body or local authority.

7 The Organisation and Scale of Production

7.1 The Division of Labour

The division of labour *increases production* because:

1. Each man is employed in the job in which his *superiority is most marked* (see also Chap. 37).
2. Learning is facilitated.
3. Economy of tools permits *specialised machinery*.
4. *Time* is saved through not having to switch operations.
5. Costs and output can be *estimated* more accurately.

But there are *disadvantages*:

1. *Monotony of work* may lead to inefficiency.
2. The risk of *occupational disease* is increased.
3. A *reduction in demand* presents difficulties when skills are highly specialised.
4. Greater *dependence of workers* on raw material or component suppliers.
5. *Standardisation* of product.

The *extent of the division of labour* depends on: (*a*) the number of workers available; (*b*) continuity of same operation; (*c*) an exchange system; (*d*) the size of the market.

7.2 The Advantages of Large-scale Production

Internal Economies

Internal economies are those which a firm can achieve directly by increasing its output. They are:

1. *Technical*: (a) increased division of labour; (b) specialised machinery; (c) large machines; (d) economies of linked processes. Technical economies fix the size of the *producing* unit, but the firm may contain many such units because other types of economy are possible.
2. *Managerial*: (a) full use can be made of managerial abilities; (b) specialist managers can be employed.
3. *Commercial*: (a) bulk buying; (b) selling staff worked to capacity; (c) one product may advertise others; (d) specialist buyers and sellers.
4. *Financial*: because a large firm offers banks better security and its shares are more liquid, it can raise capital more cheaply.
5. *Risk-bearing*: (a) better reserves to withstand losses; (b) diversified products; (c) many markets and sources of supply.

External Economies

External economies may occur as the *industry* grows in size. They can be economies of:

1. *Concentration*: skilled labour force, common services, roads and social amenities, technical colleges, ancillary firms. If these outweigh the disadvantages of concentration, e.g. traffic congestion, they lower costs and so influence a firm's location decision (see Chap. 9, 'acquired advantages').

2. *Common information services.*
3. *Specialist component firms.*

7.3 The Size of Firms

'*Horizontal integration*' occurs where firms producing the same product combine under the same management.

'*Vertical integration*' consists of the combination of firms engaged in the different stages of the production of a good.

'*Lateral integration*' occurs where one firm takes over another to increase the range of its products.

A '*holding company*' is one which has a controlling interest in many firms trading as separate units.

7.4 The Predominance of the Small Firm

In the UK: (*a*) nearly 90 per cent of manufacturing firms have less than 100 employees; (*b*) small firms form an even higher percentage in agriculture, retailing, construction and services. Reasons exist on both the demand and supply sides.

Demand

Large-scale production is not *economically* efficient where *demand is small* because of: (*a*) only a local demand; (*b*) transport costs; (*c*) highly specialised goods; (*d*) product differentiation.

Supply

Even where demand is large, supply considerations may limit the size of a firm: (*a*) institutional, e.g. lack of finance, government monopoly policy; (*b*) vertical disintegration is possible; (*c*) limitations of owner-manager; (*d*) being one's own boss compensates for lower profit; (*e*) diseconomies of scale when personal attention to detail, quick decisions and personal contacts are essential.

8 The Distribution of Goods to the Consumer

8.1 The Scope of Production

A manufacturer has to decide how his goods shall be distributed to the consumer. He may prefer to leave this to specialist firms – the wholesaler and retailer, representing forward vertical disintegration.

8.2 The Wholesaler

In buying in bulk from producers, and selling in small quantities to retailers, the wholesaler:

1. *Economises in distribution*, by reducing the number of journeys, invoices, etc.
2. *Keeps stocks*, so that consumers are supplied quickly and price fluctuations are reduced.
3. Arranges *imports*.
4. Performs *special functions*.
5. Receives *information* and gives *advice*.
6. Assists in day-to-day *maintenance* and repairs.

8.3 The Retailer

Functions: 'to have the right goods in the right place at the right time'.

1. *Stocks* small quantities of a variety of goods.
2. *Takes the goods* to where it is most convenient for customer, e.g. town centre, travelling shop.
3. Performs *special services* for customers, e.g. ordering, repairing, advising and granting credit.
4. *Advises* the wholesaler and manufacturer.

Types of Retail Outlet

1. *Independents* are mostly small shops, accounting for about one-third of retail trade. In spite of 'close-customer' advantages, they are losing ground to the multiples, etc. Voluntary chains, e.g. Spar, give advantages of bulk buying, while 'franchising' affords the advantage of selling a well-known 'brand name'.
2. *Multiples* (10 + shops) cover 50 per cent of the market. Some specialise in certain goods, while others have an extensive range.
3. *Supermarkets* are self-service stores of 200 + sq. metres concerned mainly with groceries and foods.
4. *Hypermarkets*, large (5000 + sq. metres) 'out-of-town' shopping centres, have developed slowly in the UK owing to planning restrictions.
5. *Department stores*, by buying in bulk, developing self-service and extending credit facilities, have retained 5 per cent of market.
6. *Co-operatives* (see Chap. 6).
7. *Mail order* now accounts for 4 per cent of the market, especially women's clothing and household goods.

Factors Affecting the Type of Retail Outlet

Over the past twenty years the trend has been away from the small shop towards the large organisation enjoying economies of scale and bargaining strength in buying. The reasons are:

1. *Increased income*, switching spending to processed foods and consumer durables.
2. *Increased car ownership*, providing transport for weekly purchases at cheaper suburban shop sites having parking facilities.
3. *Increase in working wives*, leading to greater demand for convenience foods and labour-saving devices, and fewer shopping expeditions made possible by refrigerators and freezers.

Thus new supermarkets are likely to take the form of discount stores, out-of-town hypermarkets, and cash-and-carry warehouses.

8.4 The Future of the Middleman

Criticisms of the Middleman

Even if wholesalers and retailers were eliminated, their functions would still have to be performed, so that there might be no difference in the price of the good. But profit margins may be too high.

The Elimination of the Wholesaler

In recent years this has been due to: (*a*) the growth of large shops which order in bulk; (*b*) the development of road transport, reducing the need to carry large stocks; (*c*) manufacturers seeking control over retail outlets;

(d) branding of goods. In addition, a wholesaler is not used when: (e) the goods are of high value; (f) producers and retailers are in close contact; (g) the manufacturer does his own retailing.

Wholesalers have adapted through cash-and-carry warehouses and discount stores, buying in bulk and selling to retailers and the public.

Direct Selling by the Manufacturer

This occurs where: (a) he wishes to push his product or ensure standards of service; (b) the personal element is important, e.g. tailors; (c) he is a small producer-retailer serving a local area; (d) the range of output is sufficient to stock a chain of shops; (e) the product is highly technical or specially designed.

9 The Location of Production

9.1 The Advantages of Different Localities

1. *Natural*: (*a*) Accessibility to raw materials and markets. With weight-losing production, transport costs are saved by producing where raw materials are accessible. With weight-gaining industries, it is cheaper to produce near market. (*b*) Climate. (*c*) Cheap, unskilled labour.
2. *Acquired or man-made*: supply of skilled labour, communications, marketing organisations, ancillary industries, training schools, reputation.
3. *Government-sponsored*: help to firms in 'Assisted Areas' (see Chap. 35).

9.2 The Level of Rents in Different Areas

Firms compete according to the *net* revenue advantages of a site, and they have to pay the 'opportunity cost' – what the next-best use will pay. The firm which values the site the highest can pay the most. Thus it is *relative* advantages which decide land use.

9.3 Conclusions

A firm will normally choose a site where benefits are

greatest compared with costs. Acquired advantages may reinforce natural advantages, but many non-economic reasons may decide location, e.g. chance, inertia, preferences of directors, their wives or key workers.

10 Combining the Factors of Production

10.1 The Law of Diminishing Returns

This 'law' shows how *physical* yields vary as factors of production are combined in different proportions.

Assume: (*a*) two factors; (*b*) all units of the variable factor are perfect substitutes for each other; (*c*) no change in techniques or organisation.

The *law: if one factor is held fixed, but additional units of the varying factor are added to it, eventually the extra output resulting from an additional unit of the varying factor will become successively smaller.*

If land is the fixed factor and labour the variable factor, *marginal output* is the addition to total output obtained by increasing the labour force by one man. Marginal output equals average output when average output is at a maximum.

Important Points

1. Marginal output falls (that is, total output increases at a decreasing rate) because labour is an imperfect substitute for land, *not* because less efficient labour is being employed.

2. One factor must be held fixed, otherwise we have a change of *scale*.
3. The law does not apply where factors have to be combined in *fixed proportions*.
4. The law states *technical* not economic *relationships* since it tells us nothing about the relative prices of the factors.
5. *Techniques do not change.*

Practical Applications

1. It explains the low standard of living of those countries where there is a *pressure of population* on land.
2. It shows how the firm can adjust the *marginal yield* of a factor.
3. It explains rising *marginal cost curve* (see Chap. 11).

10.2 The Optimum Combination of Variable Factors

The firm seeks to obtain the maximum output from a given money outlay. Therefore:

1. Last £ spent on any factor must give the same money yield; *or*

2. $$\frac{\text{marginal product of } A}{\text{price of } A} = \frac{\text{marginal product of } Z}{\text{price of } Z}$$

Thus a rise in wages, other things being equal, will produce a substitution of machines for labour. Where land is cheap relative to labour, we have *extensive* agriculture; where land is relatively dear, *intensive* agriculture.

11 Deciding on the Most Profitable Output

11.1 The Costs of Production

Costs as Alternatives Foregone

The economist considers costs from the point of view of opportunity cost – the best alternative forgone. This bears on: (*a*) his concept of 'profits'; (*b*) production in the short period.

Profit

Supernormal profit is the total revenue
less explicit costs
less implicit costs (e.g. own labour and capital)
less normal profit (the minimum return necessary to retain a firm in the particular industry).

Fixed and Variable Costs

Fixed costs are those costs which do not vary in direct proportion to a firm's output. They are the costs of the indivisible factors and are incurred whatever the output.
Variable costs are those costs which vary directly with

output, e.g. operative labour and raw materials.

The distinction differs with time: as time increases, more factors become variable. It has two uses:

1. To distinguish between the short period and the long period. The *short period* is when at least one factor is fixed, so that the firm cannot achieve the best possible combination of factors. Only in the *long period*, when all factors are variable, can supply make a full response to a change in demand.
2. In the short period production will continue as long as *variable costs* are being covered. Fixed factors, which cannot be reduced, have no opportunity cost in the short period.

11.2 How Do Costs Behave as Output Expands?

Relationship Between Costs of Production and Diminishing Marginal Product

Because of diminishing returns, the cost of producing an extra unit of output (marginal cost) will eventually rise. The marginal product is maximum when the marginal costs (*MC*) is minimum.

Cost schedules for each output can be obtained for: *total cost* (*TC*) which equals *fixed costs* (*FC*) + *variable costs* (*VC*) of *n* units; *average fixed cost* (*AFC*); *average variable cost* (*AVC*); *marginal cost* (*MC*) of the *n*th unit.

Note: (*a*) *AFC* and *AVC* added vertically give *ATC*;
      (*b*) *AFC* is rectangular hyperbola;
      (*c*) *MC* cuts *ATC* and *AVC* when both are at a minimum;
      (*d*) minimum *AVC* occurs at a smaller output than minimum *ATC*, because *ATC* is still falling when *AVC* has begun to rise owing to falling *AFC*.

11.3 Perfect Competition

Necessary conditions:

1. *A large number of relatively small buyers and sellers* so that each is a *price-taker*, the seller facing a perfectly elastic demand curve, the buyer, a perfectly elastic supply curve.
2. *Homogenous product*, with no product differentiation (see Chap. 16).
3. *Perfect knowledge* of: (*a*) prices being asked; (*b*) profits being made.
4. *Free entry*, so that: (*a*) the number of sellers remains large; (*b*) profit (loss) being made attracts (forces out) firms.
5. *Perfect mobility* of factors (including entrepreneurship) in the long period.
6. *No transport costs*.

11.4 The Short-period Equilibrium Output of the Firm Under Perfect Competition

The Equilibrium Output

In order to maximise profit, the *equilibrium output* of a firm will be where the difference between total revenue (*TR*) and *TC* is greatest. This occurs where *MR* (the revenue received from an *extra* unit) equals *MC* (the cost of producing an *extra* unit).

While, under perfect competition, *MR* is the price and is constant, *MC* eventually rises because in the short period there are fixed factors leading to diminishing returns.

The Short-Period 'Shut-down' Price

A firm will continue producing in the short period provided variable costs are covered. By definition, fixed factors cannot be transferred, so the opportunity cost of employing them is nil. The *'shut-down'* price is at minimum *AVC* (£135, Fig. 11.1). (In the long period price must at least equal minimum *ATC*, £300 – the *break-even* price.)

11.5 The Long-period Equilibrium of the Firm and Industry

In the long period all factors are variable. Thus: (*a*) the firm can vary the size of its *plant*; (*b*) a firm can enter (or leave) the industry.

The Firm

The firm can alter the *scale* of output. At first it may have *increasing* returns to *scale* (Chap. 7). Eventually *decreasing* returns to *scale* set in as management diseconomies outweigh any other economies still being secured.

Optimum Size of the Firm

The optimum (most efficient) size of the firm is where long-period *ATC* is at a minimum. This optimum size varies from one industry to another (cf. car-production and farming).

The Industry

Where a firm is more efficient than others, it will be making super-normal profits. In the long period, new firms will be attracted into the industry by these super-normal profits, and they will copy the methods of the most

FIGURE 11.1
The Equilibrium Output of the Firm under Perfect Competition

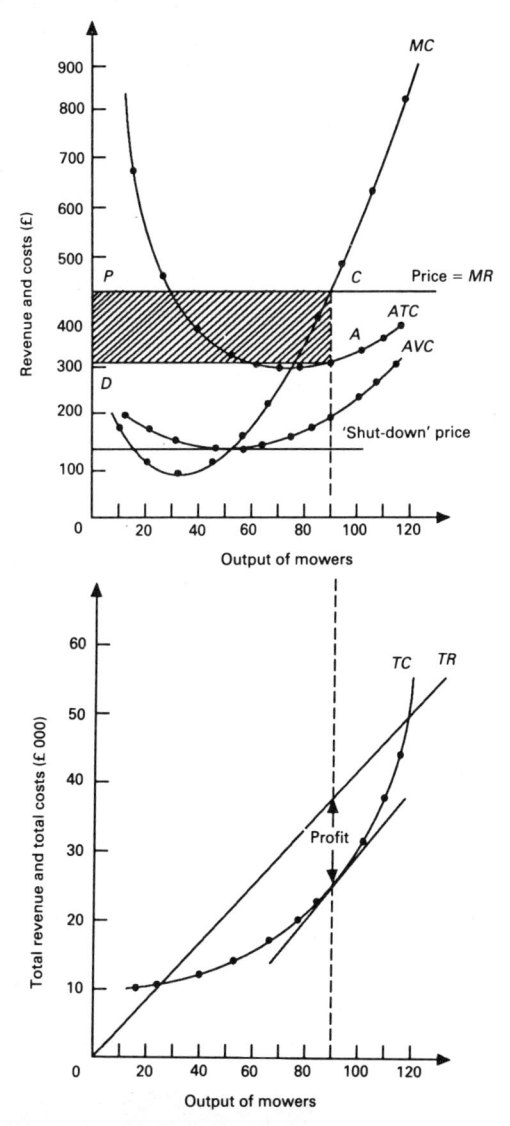

efficient firm. This increases the supply and lowers the price of the product.

Equilibrium will be achieved only when no firms are making super-normal profits because each firm is producing at the optimum size (minimum ATC) and the price of the product equals the long-period minimum ATC.

12 The Supply Curve of the Industry Under Perfect Competition

12.1 Introduction

The supply curve of the industry is the sum of the supply curves of the firms comprising the industry – in this case the group of firms producing an identical good. The industry supply schedule usually shows more being supplied the higher the price. The reason differs for the short and long periods.

12.2 The Short Period

Here the industry supply curve consists of the firms' MC curves. It rises because each firm is eventually subject to diminishing returns as output increases.

12.3 The Long Period

In the long period, each firm will be producing at its

optimum size, where price equals minimum *ATC*. This would suggest a horizontal supply curve. However, in practice:

1. *Prices of factors to the industry as a whole rise as output increases*, eventually offsetting any external economies resulting from a larger industry.
2. *Top-class entrepreneurs are not equally available to all firms*, so that some firms will always be doing better than others. This means that a higher price will bring forth an increased supply, since increasingly inferior entrepreneurs can produce.

12.4 Elasticity of Supply

Definition: the elasticity of supply of a good at any price or at any output is the proportional change in the amount supplied in response to a small change in price divided by the proportional change in price. Elasticity of supply is *elastic* if greater than 1, and *inelastic* if less than 1.

Limiting Cases

1. *Elasticity of supply equal to infinity* applies where:
    (*a*) a producer can obtain an unlimited supply of a factor at a given price; *or*
    (*b*) production takes place at constant cost.
2. *Elasticity of supply absolutely inelastic* because the good is fixed in supply whatever the price offered.

Factors Determining Elasticity of Supply

1. The period of time:
    (*a*) *Momentary equilibrium*, where supply is fixed, although stocks may be drawn on or a firm may switch factors from one product to another.

(b) *Short-period equilibrium*, where supply can be adjusted by altering the variable factors.

(c) *Long-period equilibrium*, where all factors can be changed and supply fully adjusted.

Supply is most elastic in the long period because firms can obtain their best factor combination.

2. *The relationship between the individual firms' minimum supply points.* If the entry of firms is spread over more or less the same minimum price, supply will tend to be elastic at that price, and vice versa.

3. *The cost of attracting factors from alternative uses.* Higher rewards have to be paid to attract factors to expand output. What is the elasticity of supply of *factors*? It depends upon: (a) the degree of substitution of the other factors, both physically and pricewise; (b) the elasticity of demand for the alternative goods the factor produces (see Chap. 20).

Practical Uses of Elasticity of Supply

1. To analyse *the effect on price and output* of a change in the conditions of demand.
2. To analyse *the effect of taxes*: (a) if a good is absolutely inelastic in supply, a tax will have no effect on the amount offered for sale; (b) relative elasticities of supply and demand determine the incidence of a selective indirect tax as between consumers and producers (see Chap. 36).

13 Rewarding the Factors of Production: the Marginal Productivity Theory of Distribution

13.1 Introduction

How the product is distributed depends upon the rewards the various factors of production receive. We study: (*a*) the price of the *service* rendered by a factor; (*b*) the price of factors of production in a *particular* industry, occupation or district.

13.2 The Marginal Productivity Theory: Perfect Competition

The marginal productivity (*MP*) theory is primarily concerned with the demand for factors. Under perfect competition, an employer will pay the factor a reward equal to the full value of its contribution to the product.

The demand of the individual firm for a factor is a *derived demand* since the factor is not wanted for its own sake, but for what it can contribute to production. Thus demand depends upon the addition to receipts from employing an extra unit of the factor. *Assume*: (*a*) perfect competition in the *product* market; (*b*) perfect competition in buying *labour*; (*c*) all *workers homogeneous*; (*d*) only labour is a *variable* factor.

The above assumptions give a diminishing *MP* as extra labour is employed. Since the price of the product is constant (perfect competition) there is a *diminishing* marginal *revenue* product (*MRP*). Thus labour will be employed up to the point where the wage rate equals the *MRP*. Since the *MRP* is falling, more will be demanded the lower the wage rate.

Possible difficulties: (*a*) with certain factor services, e.g. police, the *MRP cannot be measured* – though employees have to proceed as if it can; (*b*) some factors have to be combined in *fixed proportions*, so that the contribution of each cannot be ascertained.

13.3 The Determination of the Price of a Factor Service

Price is determined by *demand* and *supply*.

Demand

The *position* of the demand curve of the individual firm depends upon:

1. The *physical productivity* of the factor.
2. The *price of the product* that the factor is producing.
3. The *prices of other variable factors* employed by the firm, since factors will be combined so that:

$$\frac{MRP_A}{P_A} = \frac{MRP_Z}{P_Z}$$

The shape of the demand curve and imperfect competition are considered later.

The *industry's demand curve* is the sum of the demands of the individual firms. If we assume that the price of the product falls as the industry's supply increases, there will be a downward-sloping demand curve for a factor.

Supply

Normally a higher reward will attract factors from other industries, but the actual shape of the supply curve will vary with: (*a*) the *nature* of the factor; (*b*) *time*.

Demand, Supply and Price

The reward of a factor service (its price) is determined by the interaction of demand and supply. If the price of the product rises, the *MRP* of the factor increases, and so the price of the factor service rises.

Imperfect Competition and Factor Rewards

Where a firm sells its product under imperfect competition or is the only employer in a locality, its demand for the factor will be less than if there were perfectly competitive conditions. Trade unions may also be monopolies in the sale of labour.

13.4 Weaknesses of the Marginal Productivity Theory

1. In practice an employer may know only the *expected MRP*.
2. *Inflexibility of the wage rate* results in unemployment.
3. Through *immobility*, factors may earn 'economic rent'.
4. Theory ignores *imperfect competition* in goods and factor markets.
5. *Trade union power* needs more emphasis.

Part IV

The Government and the Allocation of Resources

14 Market Failure and the Role of Government

14.1 Efficiency in the Allocation of Resources

Economic efficiency is achieved when society has attained maximum satisfaction from the allocation of its limited resources. Given certain conditions, the market can achieve simultaneous exchange, technical and economic efficiency.

Exchange efficiency: no overall increase in satisfaction can be achieved by an exchange of goods since preferences are related to market price:

$$\frac{MU \text{ of good } A}{P \text{ of } A} = \frac{MU \text{ of } B}{P \text{ of } B} = \frac{MU_A}{MU_B} = \frac{P_A}{P_B}, \text{ etc.} \quad (1)$$

A single market price will rule for each good until each consumer is in equilibrium.

Technical efficiency: no possible net increase in output by factor substitution or reorganisation because:

$$\frac{MPP_M}{MPP_N} = \frac{P_M}{P_N} \quad (2)$$

Economic efficiency: supply is related to demand, i.e. opportunity cost is reflected in money terms by marginal cost (MC), with $P_A = MC_A$; etc., giving:

$$\frac{P_A}{P_B} = \frac{MC_A}{MC_B} \quad (3)$$

From (1) and (3),

$$\frac{MU_A}{MU_B} = \frac{P_A}{P_B} = \frac{MC_A}{MC_B}$$

That is, through relative prices, people's preferences are related to the cost of supply.

14.2 How Does Market Failure Arise?

For efficiency through price system, *certain conditions* must hold:

1. *Perfect competition*, which involves:
    (a) a *perfect market*;
    (b) *perfect knowledge*;
    (c) $P = MR$, and firms produce where $MR = MC$;

(d) *increasing costs*;
(e) perfect *factor mobility*;
(f) all the above exist *simultaneously*.
2. No *externalities*.
3. All goods can be *priced* in the market, excluding 'free-riders'.

Government *intervention* seeks to:

1. *Remedy misallocation* through market failure;
2. improve *economic stability*.

14.3 Economic Functions of Government: a Summary

1. *Allocation of resources*, remedying the above defects of the market economy.
2. *Stabilisation of the economy* to achieve:
    (a) full employment;
    (b) stable price level;
    (c) balanced regional development;
    (d) healthy balance of payments;
    (e) satisfactory growth rate.
3. *Redistribution of income*, though effect on welfare cannot be measured scientifically.

14.4 The Value of 'Perfect Competition' Analysis

1. *Simplifies*, and conclusions can eventually be modified.
2. A more *realistic* initial set of assumptions for real world than starting with monopoly.
3. Provides an *indication of 'efficiency'* so that the government can remedy deviations, e.g. where there are external costs, or accept monopoly as being conducive to innovation, etc.

15 Monopoly

15.1 Imperfect Competition

What Do We Mean by Imperfect Competition?

Imperfect competition occurs where there is a breach of the conditions of perfect competition:

1. *Many small sellers and buyers.* Where there are only a few sellers, they may each supply so large a part of the market that the amount supplied affects the market price. Such a seller is faced with a downward-sloping demand curve. Similarly, a large buyer may be faced with an upward-sloping supply curve.
2. *Homogeneous product.* Seller controls part of the market by 'differentiating' his product or by 'goodwill'.
3. *Perfect knowledge, free entry and perfect mobility of factors.* Consumers continue to buy at a higher price through ignorance of prices elsewhere. Where factors are not mobile, they may be at the mercy of a single buyer. Both lead to less than perfectly elastic demand and supply curves.

Forms of Imperfect Competition

These range from monopoly (single seller) to monopolistic competition (an industry consisting of many firms each producing a slightly different product). In between is 'oligopoly', where there are so few sellers that each has to consider the pricing and supply policies of rivals.

15.2 What Do We Mean by 'Monopoly'?

A *theoretical* definition based on 'one seller' or on a demand curve of constant unity elasticity facing the monopolist is impossible. We therefore adopt a *practical* approach – that a single seller controls supply by excluding competitors because there are *gaps* in the chain of substitution between goods. He faces a downward-sloping demand curve.

In the UK a monopoly is said to exist if a single seller controls *one-quarter* of the market.

15.3 Foundations of Monopoly Power

Control over the supply of a good may be in either its production or sale, because of:

1. *Immobility of factors of production* through: (*a*) legal prohibition; (*b*) patents and copyrights; (*c*) government policy; (*d*) control of sources of supply; (*e*) restrictions on imports.
2. *Ignorance* of competitors of: (*a*) monopoly profits; (*b*) know-how.
3. *Indivisibilities* in production.
4. *Deliberate policy to exclude competitors* – 'contrived scarcity' (as opposed to a 'spontaneous' monopoly) by 'takeovers', combinations, price-cutting, tendering agreements, withholding vital supplies from buyers.

FIGURE 15.1
The Equilibrium Output of a Monopolist

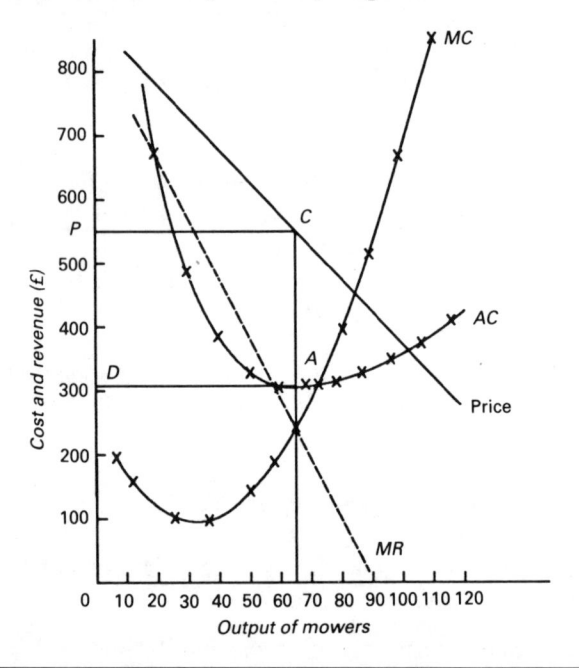

15.4 The Equilibrium Output of the Monopolist

The effect of a downward-sloping demand curve is that *MR* is always less than price at any given output (Fig. 15.1). But, to maximise profit, the monopolist still equates *MR* and *MC*, making super-normal profits of: equilibrium output × (price − average cost) = DAAC.

Important Points of Analysis

1. *MR is related to elasticity of demand* in that *MR* is

positive when demand is elastic, and negative when demand is inelastic. Therefore: (*a*) a monopolist will never produce an output where demand is inelastic; (*b*) where he has no *MC*, he will produce where *e of d* = 1; (*c*) where he has *MC*, he will always produce where demand is elastic.
2. With a straight-line demand curve, the *MR curve bisects* the horizontal distance between the price axis and the quantity demanded.
3. The greater the *absence of substitutes*, the greater is the power of the monopolist to make profits.
4. The monopolist can product an output where *MC* is *falling* even in the long period.
5. It is impossible to draw a *supply curve* for a monopolist.
6. Even in the *long period*, the monopolist can retain *super-normal profits*.

15.5 Public Policy and Monopoly

Policy Considerations

General rule: *control 'spontaneous'* monopolies; '*break up* the *deliberate*'. In practice, distinction is difficult. Moreover policy must allow for the following:

(*a*) a monopolist may not always produce a smaller output and at a higher price than under perfect competition because *economies of scale* may produce lower cost curves;
(*b*) monopoly powers may be necessary to induce *innovation and research*;
(*c*) monopoly may help *stability of output*;
(*d*) *discriminating monopoly* may allow certain markets to be supplied.

Control of Monopoly

While monopolies can be divided into '*spontaneous*' (i.e. to a large extent unavoidable) and '*deliberate*' (i.e. created to eliminate competition), the former may still restrict output to make profits, while the latter may benefit through economies of scale.

Thus policy tends to *regulate* rather than prohibit, but difficulties arise in assessing benefits and disadvantages (which may vary with circumstances), defining 'unfair competition' in legal terms, and reconciliation with other government policy.

Policy takes five *main forms*:

1. *State ownership*, so that industry works for the public interest instead of private profit.
2. *Regulation*, in order to retain the advantages of monopoly and working under private enterprise. The *Monopolies and Restrictive Practices Act*, 1984, set up a Monopolies Commission to investigate cases where one firm dominated one-third (now one-quarter) of the market.
3. *Breaking up or prohibition*, in cases where, on balance, monopoly is detrimental to consumers. Methods used include: limitation of patents, publicising profits or outlawing. In the UK minimum resale price requirements have been made illegal by the *Restrictive Trade Practices Act*, 1956, and the *Resale Prices Act*, 1964. The *Monopolies and Mergers Act*, 1965, gave the government powers to prohibit a merger if the Monopolies Commission recommended this. The *Fair Trading Act*, 1973, aimed at promoting competition by creating a Director-General of Fair Trading to monitor possible uncompetitive practices, extended the powers of the Monopolies and Mergers Commission, and reduced the criterion for monopoly

to one-quarter of supply. The *Competition Act*, 1980 sought to increase competition. With the 1993 *Single Market*, EC monopoly law will apply.
4. *Price control.*
5. *Market solutions* by:
    (*a*) *franchising*, e.g. ITV programmes;
    (*b*) *contestable markets*, e.g. opportunity to use British Gas pipelines;
    (*c*) *price regulation* by formula.

15.6 Discriminating Monopoly

Conditions: a monopolist can sell the same product at different prices to different customers because of: (*a*) imperfect competition; (*b*) different elasticities in the markets; (*c*) no 'seepage' between markets.

Equilibrium Position

1. *Total output*: where *MC* of *total* output = *MR* in each market.
2. Division of output between markets: output in each market is where *MR* = *MC* (of total).
3. *Price* is higher in the market where demand is *less* elastic.

Price discrimination may be in the interests of consumers where:

1. It permits a profit-maximising monopolist to *supply a poorer market*.
2. A *single price* would not produce sufficient *TR to cover TC*.

16 Imperfect Competition: Other Forms

16.1 Monopolistic Competition

Conditions: (*a*) *product differentiation* or *goodwill* gives a downward-sloping demand curve; (*b*) *free entry*, so that super-normal profits are eliminated in the long period.

Equilibrium of Industry

Assume: (*a*) perfectly elastic supply of factors to firms; (*b*) no external economies as the industry expands.

1. *Short period*: $MC = MR$, but super-normal profits possible.
2. *Long period*: free entry reduces price until $MC = MR$, and $ATC = price$ so that there are no super-normal profits. But price is higher than MR, and the equilibrium output is less than under perfect competition.

Economic and Social Effects

1. Even in the long period, *firms operate at less than the optimum size*, though this may be the penalty of satisfying differences in tastes.

2. *Costly competitive advertising* (as opposed to *'informative'*) to persuade people, though this may be the concomitant of freedom of choice.

16.2 Oligopoly

With oligopoly, where just a few firms comprise the industry, no definite equilibrium of output, price, etc. can be predicted since each firm has to make assumptions as to competitors' likely response to its actions. Such assumptions can differ.

The assumption that price cuts, but not price increases, will be matched gives the 'kinked demand curve' model, which predicts a range of price stability.

In practice, firms, being few, tacitly agree on maintaining prices, but often indulge in non-price competition.

16.3 Pricing Policy in the Real World

In practice, the $MC = MR$ output/pricing policy is often not adhered to because so many firms are not complete 'price-takers'. Cash-flow difficulties may limit output, while the inability to attribute fixed costs among different products means that a firm has to adopt a 'mark-up' method of pricing. The development of products is essential because of the 'product life cycle'.

17 Externalities and Cost–benefit Analysis

17.1 Externalities

Externalities (spill-overs) are the costs or benefits additional to the private costs or benefits of a transaction and which are not provided for directly in the market price. Thus social costs (benefits) = private costs (benefits) + external costs (benefits).

17.2 Methods of Dealing with Externalities

The *price system* may respond to external costs; e.g., traffic congestion may reduce the trade of a shop. Consequently *private action* may incorporate the externality; e.g., supermarkets provide parking, collective opposition to a motorway.

But *government action* may be necessary where externalities are so far-ranging that their cost/benefit cannot be allowed for by the market or private action. Such action can take the form of:

1. *Pricing*, e.g. parking meters.
2. *Taxation*, e.g. leaded petrol, or *subsidies*, e.g., for listed building repair.
3. *Physical controls*, e.g. planning requirements.

4. *Internalisation of externalities* by widening the scope of functions, e.g. The National Rivers Authority.
5. *Government provision*, e.g. slum clearance.

Environmental externalities may require *international recognition*, e.g. nuclear fall-out, the Worldwide Wildlife Fund.

17.3 Cost–benefit Analysis: Reasons for

Market prices should relate consumer demand to costs of supplying. But they *may not exist* for many government goods, e.g. roads, amenity land, or *may be defective* in that they do not allow for externalities.

Allocating resources according to political considerations results in subjective rather than objective allocation and too-centralised decision making. Cost–benefit analysis (CBA) seeks to bring *greater objectivity* into decision making by quantifying *all* benefits and costs in money terms so that they can be aggregated in a balance sheet.

17.4 Difficulties of CBA

1. While the cost of compensating losers should be included, such *losers may not be identifiable*.
2. Market prices can only be used after adjusting for any *indirect taxes/subsidies* included, or for distortion through *imperfect competition*.
3. *'Shadow' or 'surrogate' prices* are often derived from inferior sources, e.g. for a motorway, in time saved, accident reduction, increased noise.
4. Should 'shadow prices' be regarded as *equivalent to actual prices* in compiling the balance sheet?
5. What should be the *cut-off point* for *externalities* and for the *time-horizon*?

6. What *rate of interest* should be chosen for discounting future benefits/costs to obtain present values? For public projects, a *social time preference* rate lower than the current market rate should be applied.

17.5 Assessment of the Role of CBA

The use of CBA may be limited where *political considerations* are dominant in decision making, e.g. in assessing the 'social' benefits of a scheme. Nor can a firm CBA decision be taken where the decision is *irreversible*, e.g. one involving the survival of an animal species. Yet in spite of its weaknesses CBA does *provide an agenda* embracing all the issues relevant to the ultimate decision.

18 The Environment: Conservation and Pollution

18.1 The Environment as an Economic Good

The environment provides a *flow of goods and services*: (*a*) materials and energy; (*b*) space for production and recreation; (*c*) enjoyment of the 'natural world'; (*d*) a 'sink' for waste products.

But natural resources are finite; '*scarcity*' means that the way we use them involves an '*opportunity cost*'; e.g. dumping chemicals can destroy land for agriculture. Thus conservation and the control of pollution are essential.

18.2 Conservation

Because the pure market economy reflects private costs and benefits, government action is necessary to allow for externalities and the limited time-horizon of individuals when using natural resources, especially those which are non-renewable. Policy is wide-ranging – e.g. green belts, national parks, animal and bird protection, preservation of historical buildings – and provides for both renewable and non-renewable resources.

18.3 Maintaining the Stock of a Renewable Resource: Fish

Here conservation must limit what is harvested in order to maintain a stable stock since over-fishing results in an ever-diminishing stock. This arises because there are *no private property rights* over fishing-grounds so that no one fisherman can gain by limiting his catch.

This means that, to maintain a *sustainable stock*, catches of fish have to be restricted by an overriding authority or by collective agreement. Possible *methods* are:

1. *Vesting fishing rights in a single body* which owns all the fishing fleet.
2. *Physical control*, e.g. enlarging mesh size, requiring boats to remain in harbour for so many days a year.
3. *Taxing catches* at so much per tonne according to the type of fish.
4. *Quotas* for each ship, but allowing quotas to be traded in a 'quota market'.
5. *Subsidies to decommission* fishing boats.

18.4 Preserving a Non-renewable Resource: an Historic Building

Possible Weaknesses of the Market Solution

Not only is a decision to demolish a unique building *irreversible*, but it may be based on *defective market criteria*. If left to the market forces of demand and supply, the building would be demolished when its value becomes less than that of the cleared site plus the cost of rebuilding to the best alternative use, e.g. offices.

But *demand* criteria may be defective in that:

1. *external benefits* are not allowed for;
2. they ignore a possible '*option demand*' – people may be willing to pay something just to postpone a decision to demolish;
3. the present capital value of the building would be greater if, recognising society's longer time-horizon, the *social time preference rate of discount* were applied rather than the higher private time preference rate;
4. *rising future real income* may increase the demand for historical buildings (as with National Trust buildings).

On the other hand, an increase over future years in the *supply* of the alternative use (offices) would cause value to fall, with a consequent fall in the value of the cleared site. Thus, while the value of the historic building is likely to rise, the value of the cleared site declines. *Preventing immediate demolition* therefore allows for the possibility that the value of the historic building might eventually exceed the value of the cleared site.

Government Preservation Policy

Government intervention can take different forms:

1. *Public ownership*, especially where the cost of excluding 'free-riders' is prohibitive, e.g. Hadrian's wall.
2. *Subsidising* the private owner through repair grants or tax concessions.
3. '*Listing*' the building, so that official consent is required for alteration or demolition. But this is only a 'stop-gap' measure until (4) can be agreed.
4. Permit the building to be *adapted to a more profitable use*, e.g. offices, while preserving its distinctive features. This avoids a charge on public funds.

18.5 Pollution

Aspects of Pollution

Pollution results when the introduction of waste matter causes damage to the environment. While pollution occurs through *consumption*, e.g. with litter, it is that resulting from *production* which is more serious (e.g. acid rain, smoke, gases, toxic chemicals, noise) because it can affect every aspect of living.

In the last century pollution has increased with the growth in population, production and industrialisation, yet it is *growing prosperity* which not only leads to the recognition of the *problem* of pollution, but can provide the means to combat it.

To a limited extent some residuals, e.g. carbon dioxide gas, can be *transformed by the environment*, e.g. trees, into harmless or beneficial materials, e.g. oxygen. *Pollution occurs when the flow of waste residuals exceeds the natural environment's ability to assimilate it.*

In time technological developments may, while producing growth, *contain pollution* – through degradable products, efficient production reducing waste, on-site treatment of waste and 'greener' sources of energy, e.g. natural gas, wind and tide, replacing coal and oil.

The Economist's Approach

The economist must examine the problem in the context of *existing technology*. In most cases pollution represents *external costs*, so that marginal social cost exceeds private cost. Thus in Fig. 18.1, a chemical manufacturer would produce chemicals up to the point *OC* if there were no cost for discharging waste into the river. But *spill-over costs* raise the *marginal social cost* so that *OD* is the socially efficient level of production.

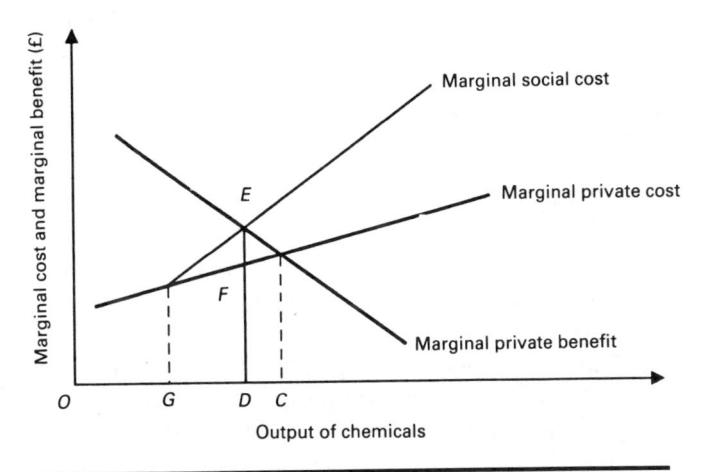

FIGURE 18.1
Efficient Output with External Costs

Policy difficulties may arise because of the weaknesses of 'shadow' pricing in measuring intangible benefits lost, e.g. natural beauty. Moreover, since pollution differs in form and scale, different measures have to be applied.

Possible Policies

1. *'Greening' public opinion* to support waste recycling and energy saving.
2. *Setting up an 'Environment Protection Agency'*, e.g. the National Rivers Authority, in which property rights can be vested in order to internalise externalities.
3. *Market negotiation* to avoid pollution, e.g. Sweden helps Poland to reduce acid rain.
4. Imposition of a *maximum standard of pollution*, though this tends to become the target, involves

inspection, and does not allow for local differences. But control is essential where pollution is dangerous to human life or is cumulative.
5. *Subsidies towards pollution reduction* through the government itself assuming removal of the source (e.g. litter). Here the cost is borne by the taxpayer, not the polluter.
6. *Taxes on pollution* (e.g. unleaded petrol). In Fig. 18.1 a tax *EF* would reduce production to *OD*. The tax can be flexible according to circumstances and encourages the installation of pollution control where the cost of this is less than the tax. Here the polluter pays, and the tax can be used to compensate losers where these can be identified.
7. *Tradeable permits*. In Fig. 18.1 if output represents the total of all chemical producers on a river and the government wishes to limit pollution to *GD*, it can give or sell licences to emit a share of *GD*. These permits are traded on the permit market, enabling firms who are pollution-efficient to sell to the least efficient, using the proceeds to achieve greater efficiency. By itself buying up permits, the government can force firms to improve efficiency.

It has to be recognised that a '*sustainable earth*' requires international agreement. This could be promoted through a United Nations 'environment protection agency' having global powers, and by the richer nations providing *funds* to the adversely affected *poorer nations*, e.g. to maintain rain forests.

19 The Provision of Goods and Services by the Public Sector

19.1 The Case for Public Sector Provision

The government provides goods and services instead of, or in addition to, the market.

1. *Community goods*, e.g. defence, street lighting, flood control, because: (*a*) they are not divisible according to individual preferences; (*b*) there is non-excludability for 'free-riders'.
2. *Collective goods* which, although indivisible, can exclude 'free-riders' by fees or tolls, e.g. parks, museums, motorways, bridges. These are usually provided free because: (*a*) *collection costs* relative to revenue are high; (*b*) they exhibit '*non-rivalry*' since use by one person does not impose a sacrifice on others; that is, because $MC = 0$, benefits are only maximised when $MR = 0$.
3. *Merit goods*, e.g. education, health care, to ensure adequate consumption, otherwise external costs could result. There may be no charge, e.g. vaccination.
4. *Internalisation of widespread externalities*, e.g. urban

renewal, or where large initial capital is required, e.g. Airbus development.

19.2 Accountability v. Economic Efficiency

The *government department* achieves maximum *accountability* through ministerial responsibility, questions in Parliament, Treasury control of finance. But for nationalised *commercial* operations this may impair *economic efficiency*.

The *public corporation* is subject to ministerial control only over broad policy and to an annual report to Parliament.

Quasi-government bodies, e.g. the National Parks Commission, the Charity Commission, operate *particular services* with minimum accountability.

Local authorities provide goods and services, and these can reflect local conditions and preferences.

19.3 The Problem of Assessing 'Needs'

Whereas '*demand*' reflects an economic willingness to pay, '*needs*' represents the subjective (often political) assessment of what society considers is an adequate standard for certain *essential goods* (e.g. housing). But standards set still have to reflect an '*opportunity cost*' claim on the limited public purse.

19.4 Pricing Policy

Three sources of funds are:

1. *Borrowing*: should cover only capital items, but these may in practice be included in current expenditure.

Public spending minus current income = PSBR (public sector borrowing requirement), which adds to the National Debt.
2. *Taxation*: covers community, collective and merit goods if no charge is levied.
3. *User-charges*: are appropriate where the beneficiary can be identified, as with postal services, prescription charges. Additionally, they *promote efficiency* in use and provide information to guide future *investment*.

But where price is below the free market price, some form of *administrative rationing* occurs, such as points system (e.g. housing), queuing (e.g. hip operations), lowering of quality (e.g. education, BBC TV).

Difficulties in levying user-charges occur because:
 (a) *fixed costs* may be so high that only one firm can be financially viable, which is then a *monopoly*;
 (b) if revenue has to cover costs, it is *impossible to produce where $P = MC$ if AR is above this*;
 (c) *high fixed costs* may mean that total costs cannot be covered by a *single price*. This may be overcome by (*i*) a *subsidy* (e.g. city transport), (*ii*) a *standing charge* (e.g. electricity), (*iii*) *price discrimination* (e.g. rail fares, by separating consumers and charging according to their different elasticities of demand, e.g. '*block pricing*').

19.5 The Nationalised Industries and Privatisation

Economic Arguments for Nationalisation

1. Secures the full advantages of *large-scale* production.
2. Essential for adequate *investment*.
3. *Monopoly* powers can be used in the public interest.

74 *The Government and the Allocation of Resources*

4. Guarantees the efficiency of *key industries*.
5. *Improved productivity* of employees.

Economic Problems of Nationalisation

1. The creation of such *monopolies* may *undermine consumers' sovereignty* and *mask inefficiency* by setting prices to cover costs.
2. Large undertakings give rise to *management problems*, e.g. in co-ordination.
3. *Investment* may be given priority for *political* reasons, and so 'crowd out' private sector investment.
4. Workers in vital industries may extort *inflationary wage increases*.

Reasons for Privatisation

Experience showed (especially in USSR) that the command economy used resources inefficiently compared with the market economy. In particular, the advantages claimed for 'privatising' state-owned assets are:

1. Improved efficiency through competition.
2. Freedom from political control.
3. Reduced public subsidies.
4. A one-off reduction in the PSBR.
5. Greater ability to resist inflationary trade union national wage demands.
6. Creation of a property-owning democracy, e.g. sale of 'privatisation' shares and of council houses.

Difficulties of Privatisation

Since many of the privatised industries have retained a *monopoly* position, it has been necessary to: (*1*) *foster competition* by: (*a*) permitting competing firms, e.g. British Telecom and Mercury; (*b*) franchising different firms, e.g. TV companies; (2) creating regulatory bodies, e.g. OFTEL, OFGAS, to ensure fair competition and monitor price increases. The latter may be stipulated by a *formula* which shares the benefit of efficiency and technical improvements between consumers and shareholders.

Part V

Rewards to the Different Factors of Production

20 Labour and Wages

20.1 The Nature of the Labour Force

Why Labour is Treated as a Separate Factor of Production

Labour is the effort, both physical and mental, made by human beings in production. People differ from machines in that: (*a*) the overall *supply* of labourers does not depend upon the return to labour; (*b*) effort is not *automatically* geared to the reward offered; (*c*) labour is *immobile*; (*d*) labour *combines* in trade unions; (*e*) workers can deteriorate if unemployment is prolonged. These characteristics have to be taken into account by firms in their attitude to employees and by the government in its employment policy.

The Overall Supply of Labour

The supply of labour is the number of hours of work offered. It thus depends upon:

1. The size of the *population*.
2. The *proportion* of the population which works – age distribution, custom, wage offered, numbers who can live on pensions and unearned income.
3. The *work offered* by each individual labourer, and whether a high income results in less work offered.
4. *Employment opportunities* available.

20.2 Methods of Rewarding Labour

By working for a wage, people *contract out of 'risk-bearing'*, though some element of risk may be incorporated in the wage agreement. The period of contract varies, operatives usually being paid weekly, and administrative staff monthly.

The *wage rate differs from earnings* through overtime, piece-rates or bonuses. Wage rates can be calculated on a *time or piece* basis. *Time-rates* are more satisfactory where:

(a) high-quality work is essential;
(b) work cannot be speeded up;
(c) there is no standard type of work;
(d) care of delicate machinery is necessary;
(e) output is not easily measured;
(f) there are health hazards of long hours;

(g) labour is a fixed factor;
(h) unavoidable periods of idleness occur.

But they have *disadvantages*:

(a) lack of incentive;
(b) supervision desirable;
(c) go-slow tactics possible.

Piece-rates are possible where the output is measurable and proportionate to effort made. Their *advantages* are:

(a) greater effort;
(b) the more efficient worker receives the greater reward;
(c) constant supervision eliminated;
(d) they provide interest to dull work;
(e) workers can set their own pace;
(f) group rewards develop a team spirit;
(g) they encourage improvement suggestions;
(h) costing simplified;
(i) they spread burden of overheads if output is higher.

Disadvantages:

(a) over-exertion possible;
(b) variations in local conditions (i) make *national* wage negotiations difficult, and (ii) undermine union solidarity;
(c) union loses control of the supply of labour;
(d) misunderstanding possible when part of the increased output is due to better machines;
(e) loss of control of employers over labour.

20.3 The Determination of the Wage Rate in a Particular Industry, Occupation or Locality

The marginal productivity theory merely provides a first approach to the problem of the determination of the wage rate. Allowances have to be made for the immobility of labour, trade union influence and government policy.

The Wage Rate and the Immobility of Labour

The supply of labour depends upon:

1. The *response* of existing labour to a higher wage rate: more work or more leisure.
2. The *cost of attracting labour* from alternative uses or localities. This in turn depends upon the *e of d* for the products made.
3. *The mobility of labour*. Immobility splits up the market since labour fails to respond to higher wage offers. Obstacles exist between:
    (*a*) *industries*, usually through prejudice or tradition.
    (*b*) *occupations* because of: (*i*) high *natural ability* required; (*ii*) long and costly *training* involved; (*iii*) trade union and professional *regulations*; (*iv*) *repugnance* (or pleasantness) of a job; (*v*) the *age* of a worker; (*vi*) an *unwillingness* to accept a lower wage rate; (*vii*) *discrimination* on grounds of sex, religion, etc.; (*viii*) *ignorance* of higher wage-rates elsewhere.
    (*c*) *districts*, through: (*i*) *costs* of moving; (*ii*) *finding accommodation;* (*iii*) *social* ties; (*iv*) *family* ties; (*v*) *imperfect knowledge*; (*vi*) *prejudice* against districts.

Differences in supply help to explain differences in the wage rates in different occupations and localities.

The Determination of the Conditions of Employment in the Real World

While *D* and *S* are the underlying determinants of the conditions of employment, these are also influenced by government intervention, imperfect competition in the labour market and trade union activity.

20.4 Trade Unions: the Process of Collective Bargaining

Functions of Trade Unions

These include:

1. Improvement of working conditions.
2. Education, social and legal benefits.
3. Improvement of standards of work.
4. Increases in pay by collective bargaining.
5. Co-operation with the government on economic policy.

The Process of Collective Bargaining

Normally the government encourages free collective bargaining, which works better with: (*a*) good sense on both sides; (*b*) strong trade union and employer organisations; (*c*) an accepted procedure for negotiation and settling disputes.

1. *Negotiation* takes place through:
    (*a*) *voluntary machinery*;
    (*b*) *Joint Industrial Councils*, encouraged by the government and consisting of representatives of employers and workers in the industry to consider problems;
2. *Settlement of disputes*. When the negotiating machinery fails, the Department of Employment may intervene by:
    (*a*) *conciliation*, to help parties reach agreement;
    (*b*) *arbitration*, when both sides agree;
    (*c*) *inquiry and investigation*, to establish the facts and make recommendations.

Trade Union Arguments for Wage Increases

1. A rise in the *cost of living*.
2. A *wage rise in other grades/occupations*; but wage differentials should reflect changes in the demand for or the supply of labour.
3. *Increased profits* of firm.
4. *Productivity* has increased.

Trade Union Bargaining Limitations

A strong trade union can obtain wage increases by:

1. *Supporting measures which increase the demand for labour.*
2. *Restricting the supply of labour.*
3. *Fixing a minimum wage rate*, though here the trade union is limited in that this may decrease the demand for labour. The extent varies with the conditions of competition:
    (*a*) *Perfect competition in both the product and labour markets*. In the short period an increase in wages is possible if the employer is making super-normal profits. In the long period there are no super-normal profits and, unless productivity increases, the wage rise will lead to fewer workers being employed. The amount of unemployment will depend upon the *elasticity of demand* for labour which will vary according to: (*i*) the *physical* possibility of *substituting* alternative factors; (*ii*) the *elasticity of supply* of alternative factors; (*iii*) the *proportion of labour costs* to total costs; (*iv*) the *elasticity of demand* for the final product.
    (*b*) *Imperfect competition*. Here the firm is likely to be making super-normal profits which the

trade union can seek to obtain through higher wage rates. Its success will depend upon: (*i*) its monopoly *control over the labour supply*; (*ii*) the *bargaining ability* of its leaders relative to that of employers.

20.5 The Government and Wages

Influence on Wage Determination

The government influences the wage rate through: (*a*) *minimum-wage* regulations; (*b*) *legal protection* re conditions of work, anti-sex and race discrimination, protection against unfair dismissal, redundancy payments, health and safety regulations.

Curbing Trade Union Power

Trade unions can reinforce political action with *economic sanctions*, e.g. strikes, go-slows and working to rule. From 1979 the government considered trade unions were misusing their extensive legal and advantages, which were therefore *progressively curtailed*.

21 Capital and Interest

21.1 Capital

What is 'Capital'?

Compared with income (a flow) *capital is a stock of wealth existing at any moment of time.* An individual or businessman would include titles to wealth, but the economist concentrates on wealth which contributes to production, i.e. *capital as a factor of production.*

Capital as a factor of production is defined as all producer goods and any stocks of consumer goods not yet in the hands of the final consumer. When calculating '*national capital*', care has to be taken to avoid *double counting* through including titles to capital (e.g. government debt). Allowance also has to be made for *capital abroad* owned by British residents, and vice versa. '*Social capital*' must be included.

Capital as a Factor of Production

This is *wealth made by man for the production of further wealth*. Such capital increases production by assisting labour, but we can only *accumulate* capital by *postponing current consumption*. This is difficult for poor countries.

Where capital is not being maintained, we say that it is *depreciating*.

21.2 Interest

Interest, expressed as a rate per cent, *is the price which has to be paid for liquid capital*. The *demand* for liquid capital arises because: (*a*) capital increases production; (*b*) producers cannot obtain all the capital required by forgoing present consumption.

Liquid capital is demanded up to the point where the *MRP of capital equals the rate of interest*. The sum of the individual demand curves gives the *industry demand curve*.

The *supply* of liquid funds for *one* use can only be obtained by bidding them away from alternative uses. Usually more liquid capital is available the higher rate of interest offered, but supply also depends upon: (*a*) *risk* involved; (*b*) the *period* of the loan; (*c*) the *elasticity of demand* for other products to which capital also contributes.

22 Land and Rent

22.1 'Land' and 'Rent' as General Terms

The Rent of Land in a Particular Use

In its everyday meaning 'rent' refers to payment for the use of land. As such its return is determined like that of other factor services (see Chap. 13).

The *demand* for land is a derived demand, and thus depends upon its *MRP*. On the *supply* side, land can be used in many ways and will be transferred to its most profitable use. Rent is determined by interaction of demand and supply, although in the short period: (*a*) a landlord may not be able to vary the rent in response to a change in demand or supply; (*b*) land cannot be transferred quickly.

22.2 Economic Rent – Land and Rent to the Economist

Ricardo's Views

Land was given by nature and fixed in supply. Hence land has no supply price (i.e. cost). The return to land, therefore, was simply the difference between the price of the product and the payments to other factors. Thus rent did not determine the price of the good; instead rent was determined by that price.

'Land' and 'Rent' Economic Theory Today

In the long period, land can be increased, e.g. by new farming techniques and transport developments. In any case, it has to be allocated between different uses – the main concern of the economist.

But Ricardo did underline that the return to a factor fixed in supply will vary with variations in the price of the product. Consequently: (*a*) the return to a fixed factor is purely a *surplus*; (*b*) a tax levied on the return to a fixed factor *will not alter the supply* of the factor and therefore output.

Economic Rent

Economists have extended Ricardo's concept of land to all factors fixed in supply. Hence *economic rent describes the earnings of any factor – land, labour, capital or entrepreneurship – over and above its supply price*, i.e. its transfer earnings ('opportunity cost' in our earlier terminology). The size of such economic rent depends on:

1. The *elasticity of supply of the factor*, which is affected by the period of time and the uniqueness of site or ability.
2. The *definition*: if we are looking at land as a whole, broad occupations or the industry, economic rent will be greater than for land in a particular use, a narrow occupational difference or for the firm.

Quasi-rent refers to economic rent on capital equipment in the short period, but which disappears in the long period as supply increases. Strictly, economic rent refers to permanently fixed factors.

23 Entrepreneurship and Profit

23.1 Entrepreneurship

Identity of Entrepreneurship and Risk-Bearing

Entrepreneurship consists of: (*a*) *co-ordinating* factors of production; (*b*) bearing the *risks of producing* for future demand. We can regard (*a*) as management, confining entrepreneurship to the risks of ownership.

Nature of Risks

Certain risks are insurable because they can be reduced to a law of averages. In a dynamic economy, however, there are uninsurable risks resulting from changes in the conditions of demand and supply. *Entrepreneurship bears the risks of uncertainty*.

23.2 Profit

The reward of *uncertainty bearing* is 'profit'. Unlike other factor rewards, profit may be negative, fluctuates more and is a residual. There are *different concepts* of profit:

1. Profit in its *accountancy sense* – the difference between total receipts and total costs.

2. *Normal profit* – the cost of maintaining the supply of uncertainty bearing for the particular industry.
3. *Super-normal profit* – any addition to normal profit – usually in the short period because some factors are fixed.
4. *Monopoly profit* – super-normal profit earned by a monopolist even in the long period.

23.3 The Role of Profit in a Market Economy

Profits (and losses) motivate the system. Where there is perfect competition, super-normal profit is eventually eliminated. In contrast, *monopoly profit*, earned through contrived scarcity, is an economic rent obtained at the expense of consumers. Where there is *perfect competition*:

1. Normal profit induces persons to *accept the risks* of uncertainty.
2. Super-normal profit *indicates* whether production should expand or contract.
3. Super-normal profit *encourages* entrepreneurs to increase production.
4. Super-normal profit *provides* the resources for expansion.
5. Super-normal profit *encourages* research, innovation and exploration.
6. Profits (or losses) concentrate production on the most *efficient* firms.

Part VI

Money and Financial Institutions

24 Money and the Rate of Interest

24.1 The Functions of Money

What is Money?

Money is a 'go-between' to effect exchanges. It can be *defined as anything which is generally acceptable in purchasing goods or setting debts*. To be money, a commodity does not have to be *legal tender* – currency which by law a creditor must accept in payment.

Precious metals made into coins became the usual form of money, but eventually bank-notes gained acceptability.

Functions of Money

'Money is said to have functions four,
A medium, a measure, a standard, a store.'

24.2 The Demand for Money

Because it is generally acceptable, money can be converted into other goods immediately and without cost. Of all forms of wealth, only money has this *perfect liquidity*. Thus people hold (i.e. 'demand') money balances. Keynes gives *three motives* for holding money:

1. *Transactions*: because receipts and expenditures do not coincide in time, consumers and businessmen need money to settle their everyday transactions.
2. *Precautionary*: extra money is held by consumers and businessmen to cover possible unforeseen needs.

(Money held for (1) and (2) Keynes called '*active balances*'; he suggested that it varies with the level of money income.)

3. *Speculative*: any money surplus to (1) and (2) must be held by somebody as 'idle balances'. The 'opportunity cost' of holding money is the yield forgone. More important, however, is the fact that *holding money permits speculation*. Any holder of assets must maintain (or improve) their value. We can simplify by lumping all alternative assets in '*bonds*', in this case undated government securities. If it is thought that bond prices are going to rise, it is best to buy bonds with idle balances, selling again when it is thought that the price of bonds has reached its peak. As the price rises, so more people will come round to the view that it has reached its peak and that a fall is likely to occur. Thus when the price of bonds is quite low, people

prefer bonds to money, but as the price rises they get back into money by selling bonds.

Because *the price of bonds is simply the inverse of the rate of interest*, the demand for speculative balances can be related to the rate of interest: when the rate of interest is low, people prefer to hold money; when it is high, people do not wish to hold money. Thus the speculative demand for money depends upon the *rate of interest* (and people's expectations), and is more liable to fluctuate than (1) and (2) which depend on the level of income.

Note: the demand for money and saving are different. Saving is income not spent; it adds to a person's assets. But a decision still has to be made as to the form in which those assets shall be held – money or goods or 'bonds'.

24.3 The Supply of Money

True money consists of: (*a*) coins; (*b*) bank-notes; (*c*) bank deposits on which people can write cheques. All these confer complete liquidity.

But *other credit instruments*, e.g. credit cards, bills of exchange, also act as money if only within a limited sphere. Indeed, in time most assets can be converted into money, and so possess some degree of liquidity. '*Near money*' reduces the amount of true money people feel they must hold.

The Official Definition of the Money Supply

Because it is now accepted that the supply of money can influence inflation, the government seeks to measure it as a guide to policy. There are two main classifications:

1. *Narrow money*: present *target* M_0 = notes and coin held by the public and banks, plus banks' holding of

till money and operational balances at the Bank of England.
2. *Broad money*: monitored $M_4 = M_0$ plus all private sterling deposits (sight and time) held in UK banks and building societies.

24.4 The Rate of Interest

Classical Economists' Views

The classical economists said that the price of loanable funds was determined by demand and supply. *Demand* will be greater the lower the rate of interest since less profitable projects become viable. *Supply* comes from people who postpone consumption; the higher the reward (interest) offered, the more willing will they be to postpone consumption. The rate of interest is fixed by the interaction of demand and supply. The *weaknesses of this approach* are:

1. It ascribes to the rate of interest *too great an influence* on investment and saving (see Chap. 30).
2. Since the classical economists view investment and saving as fairly stable, it *cannot explain short-term fluctuations* in the rate of interest.
3. It does not explain how *the government* has been able to influence the rate of interest.
4. It *assumes* that *all saving is lent* – there is no speculative demand for money.

Keynes's Explanation of the Rate of Interest as a Monetary Phenomenon

Saving adds to assets, but an individual still has to decide whether to hold money or bonds (in our model). At any one time, there is a stock of money and a stock of bonds, both of which must be held somewhere. If the demand to hold money falls, the price of bonds rises in the market, and vice versa. Thus an *equilibrium price of bonds* is established at which no more people wish to move from money into bonds, or vice versa. The inverse of this price of bonds is the 'pure' rate of interest.

In practice, *stocks* of both money and bonds do not vary much except over a considerable period of time. Hence changes in the price of bonds (and thus the rate of interest) come about chiefly through *changes in the demand for money*. It is the demand for money for the speculative motive, together with the supply of money, which, Keynes argues, determines short-term changes in the rate of interest.

The Structure of Interest Rates

There are many *different types of asset* within the term 'bonds'. All these assets are to some extent substitutes for each other, ranging from securities of different periods and risk to real wealth, such as property. According to their tastes, people spread their wealth among these different assets until equilibrium prices for each are established. These equilibrium prices (that is, *a structure* of interest rates) depend upon people's wishes for: (*a*) liquidity; (*b*) yield; (*c*) a hedge against inflation.

Allowing for Inflation

Keynes's model must be adjusted to allow for inflation because: (*a*) a continous increase in the money supply will cause people to expect further inflation; (*b*) asset-holders seek an 'inflation hedge' in equities and property, and this gives rise to the *'reverse yield gap'*.

Weakness of Keynes's 'Idle Balances' Concept

We cannot assume that, given no change in income, an increase in the money supply would be automatically absorbed in 'idle' balances.

Extra money could be spent on goods and services (see Chap. 33).

25 Financial Markets

25.1 The Provision of Liquid Capital

Liquid capital is required by firms and government for varying periods of time. Borrowers contact lenders through the money markets, the capital market and the joint-stock banks. Each market tends to specialise in the type of loan traded.

25.2 Money Markets

The Discount Market

This comprises those institutions dealing in bills of exchange:

Discount houses: will discount bills of exchange, usually selling them in 'parcels' to the commercial banks.

Acceptance houses: are mostly merchant banks who accept responsibility for the eventual payment of the bill in return for a small commission. A reduction in accepting business has meant that the *merchant banks* have developed other *functions* – arranging and underwriting new issues, advising on 'takeovers' and mergers, financing domestic business, paying dividends, acting as trustees and portfolio managers, and dealing in foreign exchange and securities.

Commercial banks: (*a*) provide discount houses with funds through '*money at call*'; (*b*) *hold bills* for last two months of their currency.

The Bank of England: (*a*) *issues* Treasury Bills; (*b*) acts as '*lender of last resort*' to hard-pressed discount houses.

Parallel Money Markets

These have developed to meet the needs of particular borrowers and lenders, and thereby increase liquidity.

1. *Sterling inter-bank market*, where banks lend surplus funds to banks having interest-earning outlets.
2. *Local authority market* for their deposits and bonds.
3. *Negotiable certificates of deposit market*: for certificates issued by banks and building societies to 3-month depositors.
4. *Eurocurrency market*: for deposits held by banks outside the country of origin.
5. *Other markets*, e.g. for *finance-house deposits*, *inter-company* deposits.

25.3 The Capital Market

This brings together those requiring and supplying long-term capital. Apart from such intermediaries as joint stock banks, merchant banks and venture capital specialists (see Chap. 6), there are:

1. *Insurance companies*, who have premiums to invest.
2. *Investment trusts*, where shareholders' money is invested in a number of companies.
3. *Unit trusts*, which make capital available when they take up 'rights' issues.
4. The *National Savings Bank*, which invests in government stock.
5. The *Girobank*, which carries out essential banking

services through the post office networth and a computerised centre in Bootle, Lancashire.
6. *Foreign banks*, which reflect the development of international banking and concentrate on foreign exchange dealing.
7. *Trust, pension and trade union funds*.
8. *Building societies*, which lend mostly to owner-occupiers of houses.
9. *Finance corporations*, often of a special nature, e.g. Agricultural Mortgage Corporation and Exports Credit Guarantee Department of the Department of Trade and Industry.
10. *Finance companies*, which have at times switched from hire-purchase to long-term finance.

25.4 The Stock Exchange

The Stock Exchange is a formal organisation for dealing in *existing securities*. 'Big Bang' 1986 ended fixed commissions and the 'single capacity' rule, enabling members to act in a dual capacity as agents for both clients and dealers – the 'market-makers'.

In practice, commission rates enable *brokers* to survive as retailers for the private investor. Prices are displayed on the SEAQ screen.

While speculative waves of optimism (bulls) and pessimism (bears) may cause wide swings in the price of securities, the Stock Exchange does fulfil real economic functions.

1. It *facilitates borrowing* by the government and industry.
2. It helps, through jobbers, to *even out short-run price fluctuations* in securities.
3. It *advertises* security prices.
4. It *protects* the public against fraud.
5. It *reflects* the country's economic prospects.

26 Clearing Banks

In contrast to the USA's unitary banking system, the UK has the 'Big Five', each with a network of branches and enjoying economies of scale and risk spreading.

26.1 Types of Banks in the UK

Banks vary in function and size:

1. The central bank: the Bank of England.
2. Commercial or joint-stock banks.
3. Merchant banks.
4. Foreign and Commonwealth banks with UK branches.
5. National Savings Bank.
6. The Girobank.

26.2 The Creation of Credit

Banks can lend more than the cash which has been deposited with them. Because people use cheques instead of demanding cash to settle debts, banks can extend their lending by 'creating' deposits provided they retain a safe cash ratio. Thus a cash ratio of 10 per cent would allow a bank to *create* deposits of £9000 upon an actual cash deposit of £1000, giving total deposits of £10 000.

26.3 Bank Lending

Considerations Determining a Bank's Lending Policy

To give *security, liquidity and profitability*, a bank:

(*a*) usually *requires collateral*, but does not lend if there is a high risk of default;
(*b*) *divides loans* between different types of borrowers and for different times; that is, it *maintains a 'portfolio'* of assets.

The Distribution of a Bank's Assets

In order of *liquidity* (and reverse order of profitability), the main assets of a bank are:

1. Cash.
2. Money at call and short notice.
3. Bills discounted.
4. Other market loans.
5. Investments (in government and local government bonds).
6. Advances (by overdrafts and loans mostly up to 6 months).

26.4 Modification of the Cash Ratio Approach

Today banks are more concerned with their *general liquidity* position than simply with cash. *New markets* have made certain loans so liquid that they can be regarded as 'near money'.

This is recognised by the monetary authorities who act on the whole of the banks' assets (and not just on cash) to control the banks' ability to lend.

26.5 The Effects of Recent Increased Competition

Banks have faced *increased competition* from: (*a*) *foreign banks*, especially in foreign exchange dealing and lending to companies; (*b*) *building societies*, which can now carry out many banking functions, e.g. issue certificates of deposit; (*c*) the ending of their interest rate cartel through the removal of controls on lending in 1971.

As a result, banks have had to *compete* by: (*a*) *reducing margins* between borrowing and lending rates; (*b*) *charging for* many customer *services*; (*c*) wooing *personal customers*, e.g. longer hours; (*d*) *extending business activities*, e.g. merchant banking.

27 The Bank of England (B of E)

The B of E was nationalised in 1946. It is the 'central bank' of the UK controlling, on behalf of the government, the policies of the commercial banks and other financial institutions.

27.1 Functions of the Bank of England

1. It *issues notes* according to the needs of trade, the *fiduciary issue* today having little relevance.
2. It is the *government's banker*, keeping its accounts, making 'advances', managing its debt and giving advice.
3. It is the *bankers' bank*.
4. It manages the *Exchange Equalisation Account* (see Chap. 40).
5. It *protects the gold and foreign currency reserves* by determining the short-term interest rate, exchange control (if operative), and arranging loans from other central banks.
6. It *exercises international financial responsibilities*
7. It *supervises the banking system* to ensure banks maintain adequate liquidity and are not over-exposed to exchange rate fluctuations.

8. It *manages the UK's monetary system* according to government policy by varying the *cost of credit*, the rate of interest.

27.2 Principles of Monetary Control

Approaches to Monetary Policy

Two main approaches: (*a*) *supply* of credit controlled quantitatively; (*b*) *demand* for credit controlled through the rate of interest.

27.3 Monetary Base Control

The old system of Competition and Credit Control, 1971–9 controlled credit quantitatively through:

1. *Minimum reserve ratio.* Each bank was required to observe a minimum reserve ratio (12½ per cent) of '*eligible reserve assets*' to '*eligible liabilities*', i.e. a ratio of liquid assets to deposits.
2. *Open market operations.* By selling securities on the open market, the B of E reduce the eligible reserve assets held by the banks, causing them to reduce their deposits (chiefly advances) by eight times; and vice versa.
3. *Special deposits.* Banks required to deposit with the B of E a given percentage of their eligible liabilities. Such special deposits do not count as eligible reserve assets, and their main impact is on advances.
4. *Minimum lending rate.* Since banks had ceased to fix their lending rates with reference to 'bank rate', the latter was replaced by a '*minimum lending rate*' fixed on a Friday at ½ per cent above the average Treasury Bill rate.

Other weapons were requests to banks to restrict lending, funding operations and supplementary deposits.

27.4 Rate of Interest Control: The Present System

The Discarding of Monetary Base Control

Quantitative controls: (*a*) merely postponed rise in rate of interest; (*b*) reduced competition; (*c*) caused funds to move out of the banking system to uncontrolled institutions; (*d*) weakened the monitoring role of sterling M_3.

Since 1981 the rate of interest has been used to limit the *demand* for credit. The actual rate is determined in the wholesale markets, chiefly the inter-bank market. But if the Bank can bring about a shortage of cash, it can *influence the rate*, as follows.

Competition between Banks

Increased inter-bank competition necessitates holding minimum non-earning operational cash in order to lend as much as possible. Thus open market operations by the sale of Treasury Bills leaves them short of cash, and they call in overnight loans.

This means that the Discount Houses have to sell bills to the Bank – on the Bank's terms. This allows the Bank to indicate what it considers to be the appropriate rate – chiefly the 7-day, but also the 3-month.

The Monetary Sector

This now includes: (*a*) all recognised banks and licensed deposit-takers; (*b*) the Girobank; (*c*) banks in the Channel Islands and Isle of Man; (*d*) Trustee Savings banks; (*e*) the banking department of the B of E. Current requirements, with the *abolition* of the minimum reserve asset ratio, are:

(a) *Cash ratio*: all banks and licensed deposit-takers to hold cash equal to ½ per cent eligible liabilities at the B of E.
(b) *Minimum lending rate* only to be used in exceptional circumstances, e.g. when UK left the ERM, 16 September 1992.
(c) *Special deposits* were retained and may be required for all institutions with eligible reserves of over £10 mn.

Part VII

The Government and Stabilisation Policy

28 Measuring the Level of Activity: National Income Calculations

28.1 The Principle of National Income Calculations

Our income is basically what we produce. The *national income is the total money value of all goods and services produced by the country during the year*.

Value of expenditure on output = value of *final output* =

value added by each factor = *income* of factors. Thus: *national expenditure* on *final* consumption and investment goods = *national output* of goods and services produced by all industries = *national income* (wages, rent, interest and profits) of all factors of production during the year.

28.2 National Income Calculations in Practice

General difficulties arise because of:

1. The necessity of having to make *arbitrary definitions* of:
    (*a*) *production*: includes only goods and services normally paid for;
    (*b*) *services of consumer durable goods*: excluded, except for owner-occupied houses;
    (*c*) *government services*: are all included at cost.
2. *Inadequate information*, because sources are inappropriate or information incomplete. No accurate figure can be given for real depreciation.
3. *Danger of double-counting* of transfer incomes, intermediary production, indirect taxes and stock appreciation.
4. *Overseas connections*
    (*a*) *Exports* have to be *added* and *imports* subtracted from *national expenditure*.
    (*b*) *Net income from foreign investment* has to be included.

Government Calculations of the National Income

Since calculations for the three methods vary, an 'average' figure is built up, and the difference from this is shown as a '*statistical discrepancy*' for each method.

Measuring the Level of Activity: National Income Calculations **107**

1. *National income* figures are obtained mainly from income tax returns, but: (*a*) transfer incomes have to be subtracted; (*b*) income from *government property* and government, public corporation and local authority trading surpluses have to be included; (*c*) there is no figure for the '*black economy*'.
2. *National expenditure* figures are obtained from the *Census of Distribution* (consumer goods) and the *Census of Production* (investment goods) supplemented from other sources. Indirect taxes have to be subtracted and subsidies added to convert market prices into factor cost. *Exports* are added, and *imports* subtracted.
3. *National output* can be measured by totalling the value of *final* goods and services, or the *added value* of every firm.

National income = GNP *less* depreciation.
Personal disposable income = GNP *less* direct taxes, national insurance contributions, undistributed profits, depreciation, profits and rents of public undertakings *plus* government transfers.

28.3 Uses of National Income Statistics

1. *To indicate the overall standard of living.* Allowances have to be made for: (*a*) changes in the *price level*; (*b*) an increased *population*; (*c*) the proportion of *investment goods*; (*d*) goods *exported and imported*; (*e*) the *distribution* of the national income; (*f*) changes in *leisure* and working conditions; (*g*) *quality* of goods may improve without a price increase, e.g. computers; (*h*) government spending on *defence*; (*i*) an increase in the *exchange* economy; (*j*) *social costs and*

benefits; (*k*) consumption of *irreplaceable resources*; (*l*) the '*black economy*', (*m*) payments brought about by *stress* of modern living; e.g. anti-depressant drugs.

2. *To compare living standards of different countries*. National income figures may be useful for assessing aid or UNO contributions. But there are *difficulties* additional to those of (1) above through differences between countries in: (*a*) the values of *currencies*; (*b*) *tastes* and spending; (*c*) *defence* spending; (*d*) the proportion of *women working*, the *exchange* economy and *tax return accuracy*; (*e*) the *distribution of income*; (*f*) *educational and medical* facilities.
3. *To calculate the rate at which a nation's income is growing*.
4. *To establish relationships between various parts of the economy*, e.g. between profits and investment, trend of government 'take'.
5. *To assist the government's management of the economy*
6. *To assist the private sector to forecast likely economic movements*.
7. *To indicate changes in the distribution of income*.

28.4 Factors Determining a Country's Material Standard of Living

The *standard of living* can be roughly defined as the *national income per head* of the population. It is determined by the following factors:

Internal

1. Original *natural resources*.
2. Nature of the *people*, particularly the labour force.
3. *Capital equipment* available.

4. *Organisation* of the factors of production.
5. *Knowledge of techniques*, and their application.
6. *Political stability*.

External

1. Net income from *overseas*.
2. The *terms of trade*, i.e. the quantity of imports obtained for a given quantity of exports.
3. *Gifts* from abroad, e.g. defence and aid.

29 Unemployment

29.1 The Nature of Unemployment

In 1932 the rate of unemployment in the UK reached 22.1 per cent of the working population. This experience has consistently dominated Britain's post-war economic policy, with the expansion of aggregate demand producing 'over-full' employment and resulting in inflation, etc. Government counter-inflation measures and general world depression for instance, has resulted in the UK having 2.9 million unemployed (10.5 per cent) in April 1993.

Government action to reduce unemployment is particularly necessary because of the resulting human misery. But because problems arise at a very low level of unemployment, some trade-off is essential.

Without direction of labour, complete full employment cannot be achieved. Thus in a free society the target figure is decided politically. The stated government target is likely to be about 5 per cent.

Definition: unemployment occurs when persons capable of and willing to work are unable to find suitable paid employment. But 'unemployment' must be involuntary and exclude the unemployables. To keep it to a minimum, people must be prepared to switch jobs.

29.2 The Causes of Unemployment

1. *Frictional*: in a non-static economy people will always be changing jobs. The price system may not shift labour from one place to another because of: (*a*) ignorance of vacancies elsewhere, (*b*) obstacles to movement.
2. *Seasonal*: can be reduced by having temporary, seasonal help.
3. *International*: arises because: (*a*) exports are not competitive, (*b*) customers' incomes have fallen.
4. *Structural*: results from long-term changes in the conditions of demand or supply. The problem is serious where a highly localised industry is dominant (see Chap. 35).
5. *Cyclical*: refers to the alternate booms and slumps (recessions) – the 'trade cycle' – in economic activity of the last 100 years. Caused, according to Keynes, by *inadequate aggregate demand*, which could be remedied by government action.

30 The Level of Output and Aggregate Demand: the Keynesian Explanation

30.1 The Link Between Spending and Production

We look at the *circular flow of income* (Y) in the economy as a whole. *Firms* (the producing units) pay income to *households* (the consuming units) whose spending on goods and services determines the receipts, and thus the profits of firms (Fig. 30.1). It follows:

1. The *equilibrium output* of the economy occurs where spending on goods and services equals spending by firms (including normal profit) on factors of production.
2. The *level of production* (and employment) is related to the level of spending.
3. *Spending may not be sufficient* to produce an equilibrium level of output where all factors are *fully employed*.

FIGURE 30.1
The Circular Flow of Income

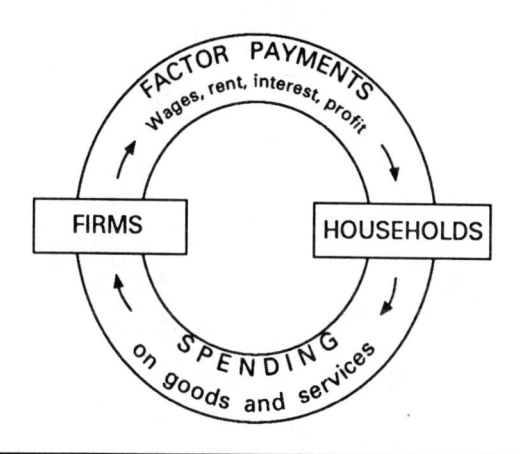

Assume: (a) Net profit is gross profit less depreciation, and all depreciation retentions are spent on replacement investment – so investment (*I*) is *net* investment; (b) all net profit is distributed; thus there is *no saving by firms*; (c) no *government* taxation or spending; (d) a *closed economy*; (e) no changes in the *price* level; (f) *employment* is directly *proportionate to output*.

30.2 Reasons for Changes in Aggregate Demand (*AD*)

National income/output (*Y*) depends on spending (*AD*). Thus we have to discover why *AD* changes.

Not all *Y* is spent (*C*) by households; some may be saved (*S*). *S* will be lost to the circular flow of income unless it is borrowed by firms for investment spending (*I*)

FIGURE 30.2
The Level of Income Maintained through Investment

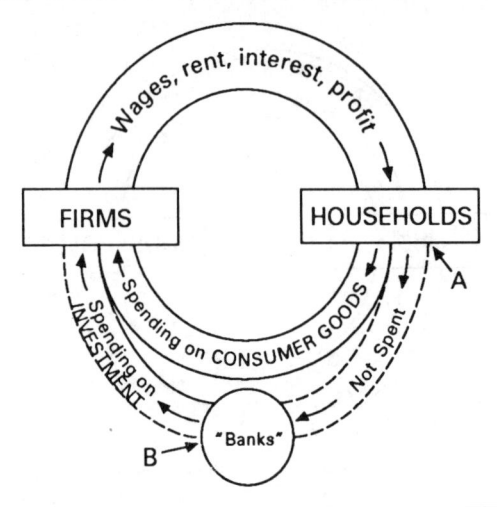

Firms → Households: Wages, rent, interest, profit
Households → Firms: Spending on CONSUMER GOODS
Households → Banks: Not Spent (A)
Banks → Firms: Spending on INVESTMENT (B)

(Figure 30.2). In a private enterprise economy, S by households can differ from I by firms. We have to consider the factors determining both.

30.3 Consumption Spending

1. *C and S by 'households': personal saving*
   $Y = C + S; C = Y - S; S = Y - C.$
   Thus S can be affected by spending decisions, and C can be affected by saving decisions (thrift). Therefore we examine the factors which influence *spending* and *thrift*.
   Spending decisions are more important in the short run since a person seeks to maintain his standard of living. They depend on:

FIGURE 30.3
The Relationship between Consumption and Income

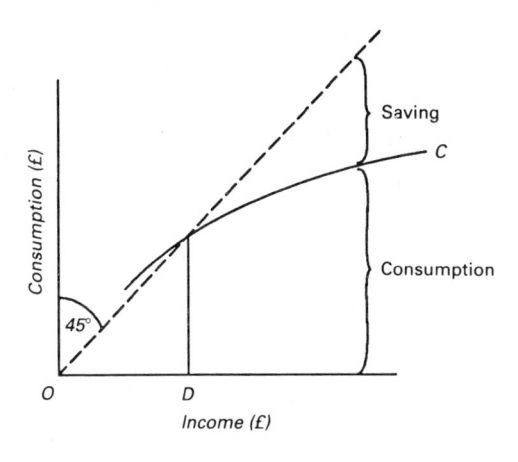

- (a) *Size of income.* At low *Y*, *C* may be greater than *Y* (from past saving or borrowing). We also note a *diminishing marginal propensity to consume*: as *Y* increases, a smaller amount of any *given* increase is spent (Fig. 30.3).
- (b) The *time-lag* in adjusting spending habits.
- (c) Changes in *disposable income*, e.g. through direct taxation, profits distribution.
- (d) The size of an individual's *wealth*.
- (e) Invention of *new consumer goods*.
- (f) *Hire purchase* and other *credit facilities*.
- (g) An anticipated *fall in the value of money*.
- (h) *Inflation*: uncertainty re government anti-inflation measures may lead to increased saving, as will the desire to restore the real value of money balances.

(i) The *age-distribution* of the population.

Thrift depends on:
- (a) Size of *income*.
- (b) The *life cycle* stage.
- (c) *Psychological attitudes*.
- (d) Social *environment*.
- (e) *Government policy*, e.g. interest rate offered, tax exemptions.

2. *Business saving*, by retaining profits, depends on:
   - (a) *Profits* made.
   - (b) *Subjective factors*, such as the desire to *equalise dividend* payments.
   - (c) Estimated *future* prices.
   - (d) *Government policy*, e.g. size of corporation tax.

3. *Government saving*, by:
   - (a) *Central government* budget surplus.
   - (b) *Public corporations'* profit retentions.
   - (c) *Local authorities'* budget surpluses.

Public sector spending is closely controlled by the government, and any surplus is mainly to combat demand inflation.

Conclusion: private C (and S) depend upon: (a) Y; (b) other, fairly stable, factors. Thus the level of AD is the main short-term cause of changes in C. This means that instability of AD must be largely caused by changes in I.

30.4 Investment Spending

Definition: gross investment is spending over a given period on the production of capital goods or on net additions to stocks. Net investment is gross investment less depreciation.

In national income calculations, I is *not* the buying of securities.

FIGURE 30.4
The Determination of the Level of Investment

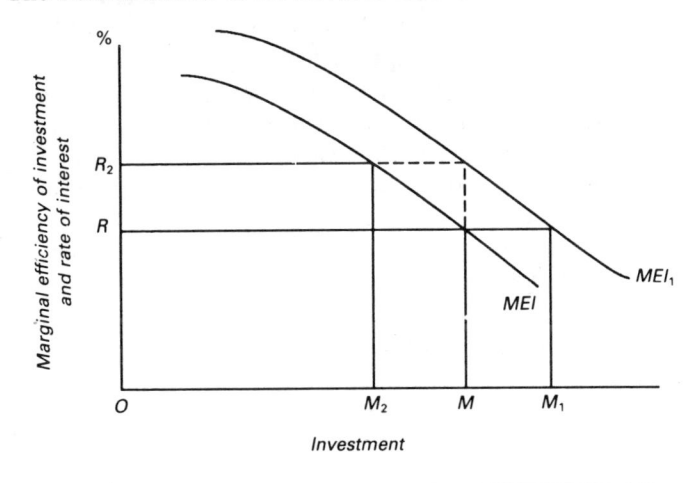

Investment in the Private Sector

Investment in the private sector is governed by:

1. *Expected yield relative to cost.* The marginal efficiency of investment (*MEI*) is the discounted expected rate of return on *I*. The *MEI* is likely to fall as the community's capital increases (through more *I*) because: (*a*) the price of the product falls, thereby reducing the yield; (*b*) the prices of factors making the capital good rise, so that its supply price rises. Both produce a lower *MEI*.

The equilibrium level of *I* occurs where *MEI* = the marginal cost, i.e. the rate of interest (Fig. 30.4).

Investment may alter because: (*a*) *expected yield alters*, which is quite likely because the views of entrepreneurs are subject to waves of optimism and

pessimism, inflation fears, political instability and changes in government policy; (b) *the rate of interest changes*, although this is not now considered to be of major significance, especially in comparison with the extent to changes in expected yield.
2. *Changes in techniques*, e.g. microchip, North Sea gas.
3. *Changes in the rate of consumption*. The *accelerator* examines I induced by changes in C, and shows that some I is linked to the *rate of change of C* rather than the actual level of C.
4. *Government policy*, e.g. restrictions on credit, investment allowances, the rate of interest.

Investment in the Public Sector

I in the public sector is fairly stable, and is linked to policy decisions rather than the rate of interest. Local authority I, however, may be affected by a rise in the rate of interest since higher costs would involve a Council Tax increase.

Public I cannot always be held back to make good a downturn in private I.

Summary

Employment depends upon the level of AD – the total amount of money spent on the goods produced. AD fluctuates according to the relationship between intended S and I, so that eventually actual S equals I.

1. AD expands if:
    (a) I increases but S remains unchanged;
    (b) S decreases but I remains unchanged.
2. AD contracts if:
    (a) I decreases but S remains unchanged;
    (b) S increases but I remains unchanged.

In practice, I is more liable to frequent change than S.

Whereas firms' expectations are highly sensitive to new conditions, households' spending habits are fairly stable.

30.5 Equilibrium Through Changes in the Level of Income (Y)

When, in an economy, what households wish to save does not equal what firms wish to invest, Y changes until intended S = intended I.

The effect of any autonomous change in I on Y will depend upon the marginal propensity to consume (c). $\Delta Y = k\Delta I$, where k is the 'multiplier' and equals $\dfrac{1}{(1-c)}$. Thus

$$\Delta Y = \frac{\Delta I}{(1-c)}.$$

This can be illustrated arithmetically on the circular flow diagram (Fig. 30.5) or diagrammatically on the 45° diagram (Fig. 30.6), where initially $Y = 1000$ and c, but I increases from 4000 to 6000.

30.6 The Effect of Changes in Consumption (C)

An autonomous change in C has, through the multiplier, exactly the same effect on the level of Y as a change in I (Fig. 30.6).

The *paradox of thrift* is that, when households seek to save more, they may end up by actually saving less. This is because the fall in AD resulting from decreased C may adversely affect the level of I, causing an even greater fall in AD. The lower Y makes households less able to maintain even former S.

FIGURE 30.5
The Effect of an Increase in the Rate of Investment on the Level of Income

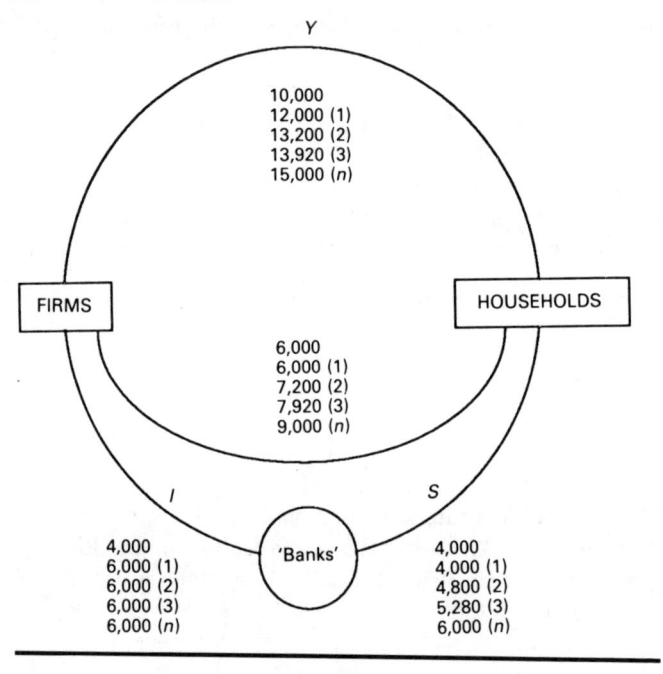

Y

10,000
12,000 (1)
13,200 (2)
13,920 (3)
15,000 (*n*)

FIRMS

HOUSEHOLDS

6,000
6,000 (1)
7,200 (2)
7,920 (3)
9,000 (*n*)

I

S

'Banks'

4,000
6,000 (1)
6,000 (2)
6,000 (3)
6,000 (*n*)

4,000
4,000 (1)
4,800 (2)
5,280 (3)
6,000 (*n*)

30.7 Government Spending and Taxation

Government spending (G) is an injection into the flow of AD similar to I, whereas taxation (T) is a leak, similar to S.

G is subject to the multiplier. But an increase in T will reduce disposable income, so that the initial reduction of C resulting from an increase in T depends upon the marginal propensity to consume out of *disposable* income. This means that a part of the burden of T will fall on an

FIGURE 30.6
The Effect on Y of a Change in I

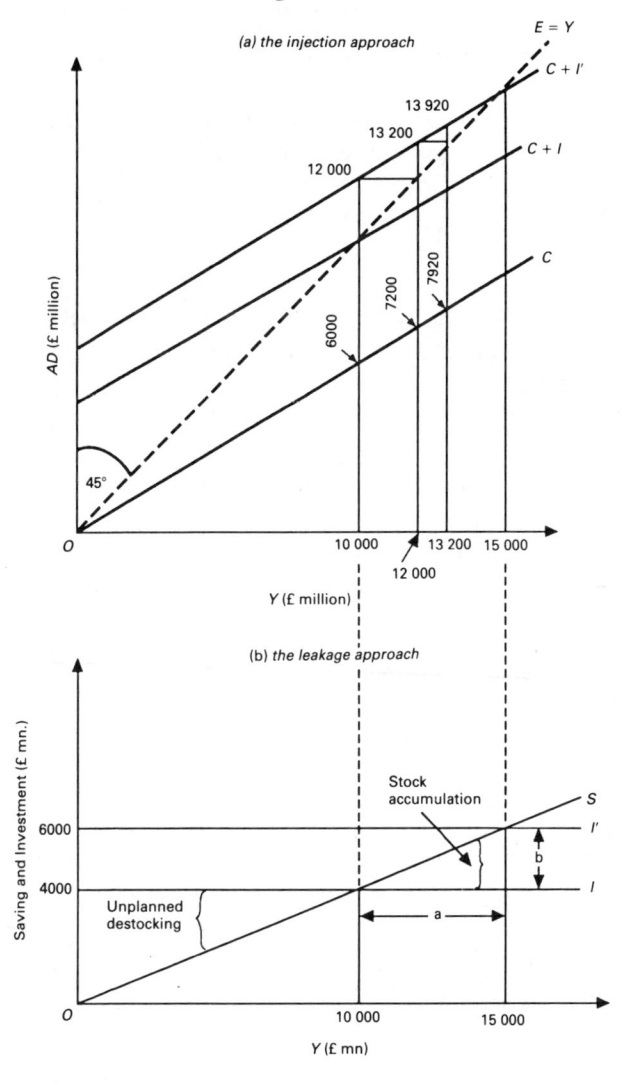

(a) the injection approach

(b) the leakage approach

existing leak – S. The initial reduction in C will be subject to the multiplier.

30.8 The Effect of Foreign Trade

Expenditure on exports (X) is an injection into the flow of AD, whereas expenditure on imports (M) is a leak. Thus:

$$\Delta AD = \frac{\Delta I + (\Delta X - \Delta M)}{1 - c}.$$

In fact, M tends to be related to Y, m being the marginal propensity to import. This will reduce the size of the multiplier:

$$\Delta AD = \frac{\Delta I + \Delta X}{1 - c + m}.$$

But a country must not try to solve unemployment by pushing X and *reducing M*.

30.9 Demand Management

Policy Implications of Keynes

Given its assumptions, the Keynesian model indicates that AD has to be maintained at the full employment level of output. This would be achieved by adjusting government spending. Thus, when there is a deflationary gap of LM (government spending = G'), G' must be increased to G.

But should there be an inflationary gap NL (G''), G'' must be reduced to G.

FIGURE 30.7
Equilibrium Levels of Income

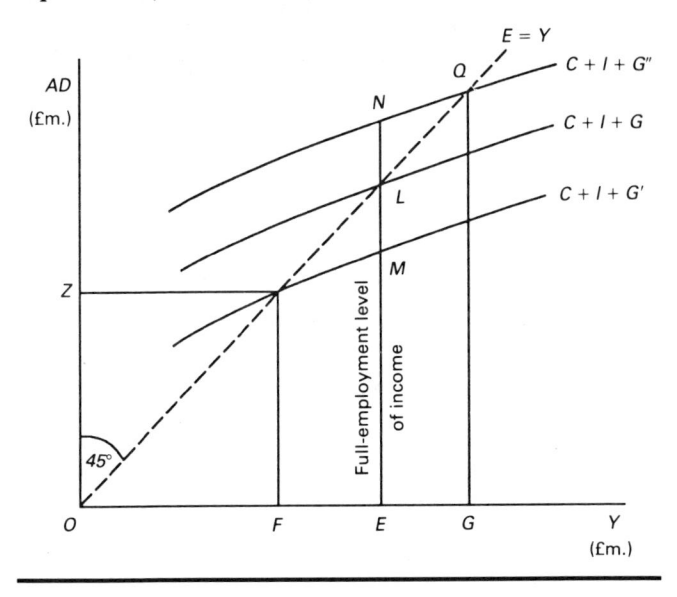

Post-war Demand Management in the UK

'Fine-tuning' AD achieved a 3 per cent unemployment rate until 1974, but it led to the difficulties of *over-full employment* – 'disguised' unemployment, under-investment, failure to innovate and develop new products, poor growth and, above all, inflation.

Weaknesses of the Keynesian Approach

1. It glossed over the *dynamic nature of inflationary pressure* as economy nears full employment, especially trade union expectations.

2. It assumed an *increase in the money supply* would go into 'idle' balances, whereas it *can add directly to AD*.
3. It failed to appreciate the impact on monetary policy of a *large PSBR* resulting from a high G.
4. It ignored the effect of a buoyant AD and inflated home prices on the *balance of payments*.

31 Employment and the Price Level

31.1 Changes in the Approach to Full Employment

'Full employment' has to be interpreted according to the government's other economic objectives, chiefly the price level. Analysis has, therefore, to consider how AD and AS (aggregate supply) are related to the price level (Fig. 31.1).

31.2 Aggregate Demand and Aggregate Supply

AD *(Planned Spending)* $= C + I + G + (X - M)$

Spending on real output is likely to expand as the price level falls because:

1. Consumers' cash balances can purchase more.
2. A reduced transactions demand for money leads to a fall in the rate of interest, encouraging higher C and I.
3. More price-competitive home-produced goods expand X and reduce M (e.g. cars).

The AS Short-run Curve

Three stages are depicted:

1. *Horizontal* at low level of output: factors can be

FIGURE 31.1
The Relationship of Output and the Price Level to *AD* and *AS*

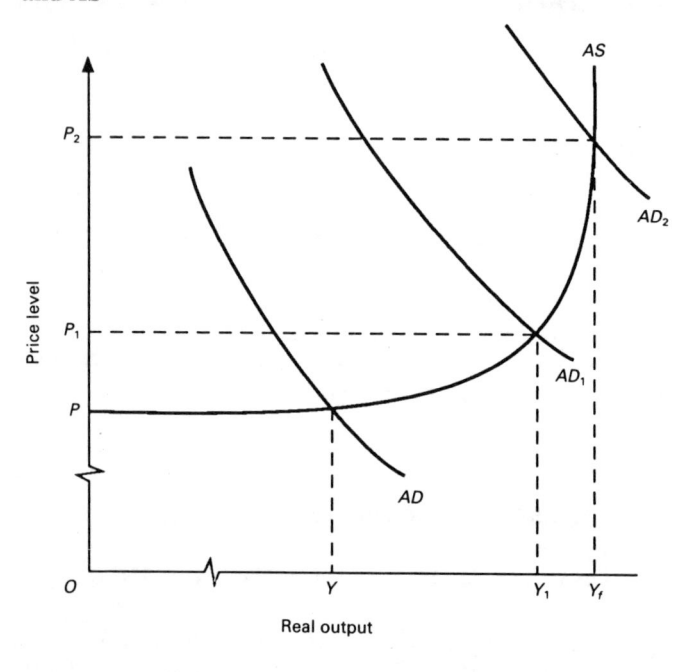

engaged at existing prices so that additional spending on inputs gives a proportional increase in output.
2. An *eventual rise at an increasing rate*: the result of diminishing returns to capital equipment, bottlenecks in components and skilled labour, and wage demands.
3. *Vertical*: at maximum potential output.

Fig. 31.1 shows an equilibrium output/price level where *AD* and *AS* intersect.

Inadequacy of Demand Management

This arises because:

1. Forecasts may be based on unreliable statistics or past human behaviour.
2. In the *short run* an increase in AD may expand employment since firms' profits rise. But in the *long run*, labour secures *wage increases* to match the rise in the price level. The resulting fall in profits causes output to revert to its original level – but at a higher price level.
3. Indeed, *labour not only adapts* from past experience, but learns how to interpret information with regard to its likely effect on the price level. It therefore secures an appropriate and commensurate wage increase immediately. Thus, with '*rational expectations*' there is no intermediate short-run employment benefit to an increase in AD (as labour 'adapts'), but simply a direct rise in the price level.

31.3 Full Employment and Demand Management

Fig. 31.1 shows that, given full employment at Y_f, an adequate AD is necessary for output to be near the full employment level but that the price level objective is also relevant. Thus *government intervention* is concerned with (*a*) how much?, (*b*) what measures? and (*c*) timing.

31.4 How the Government Can Manage AD

Fiscal and monetary measures must support one another.

Fiscal Policy

Fiscal measures cover changes in G and T to vary AD, and take the form of:

1. *Automatic stabilisers*, e.g. as AD expands, income tax and VAT yields rise; as output falls, unemployment benefit payments increase.
2. *Discretionary changes* by:
    (a) Varying the *type of tax*; e.g. reduced indirect taxes would enable poorer people to increase their spending; lower corporation tax would encourage firms' investment spending.
    (b) Changing the relationship between G and T, a larger budget deficit expanding AD, and a surplus contracting AD. But while taxes can thus allocate resources between the private and public sectors, there are snags, such as: (*i*) the convention of annual budgets; (*ii*) taxation may take time to be operative; (*iii*) taxes may not be discriminatory; (*iv*) a high PSBR can result from an expansionary budget.

Monetary Policy

By adjusting the rate of interest, the government can influence C and I through the cost of borrowing and its psychological impact. Difficulties: (*a*) a high rate may be necessary to reduce planned long-term investment – and in this case affects future growth; (*b*) a high rate discriminates against social projects deserving priority.

31.5 Supply-side Economics

If the short-run aggregate supply curve can be shifted from AS to AS_1, AD can be increased to AD_1 so that

FIGURE 31.2
Supply-side Policy

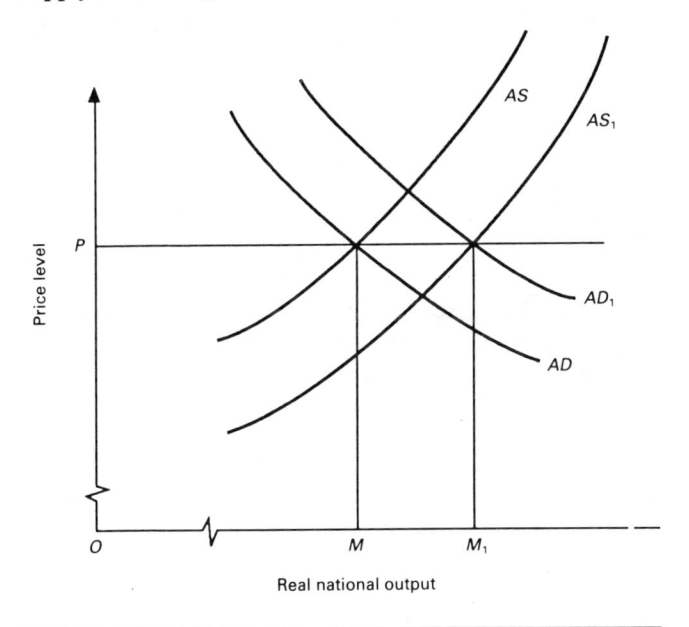

output expands from OM to OM_1 with no rise in the price level (Fig. 31.2).

Supply-side measures to lower the AS curve cover:

1. *Greater market freedom*: reducing government controls; removing minimum wage regulations; reducing trade union power; privatising public sector goods and services; improving competition, including new devices for the natural monopolies; abolishing control of capital movements abroad.
2. *Cost reductions*: through lower employers' National Insurance contributions; labour training and mobility

measures; Assisted Area subsidies; advisory services (e.g. on Single Market).
3. *Incentives*: through lower income and corporation taxes; capital availability for new firms; profit-related pay and share option schemes.

31.6 Postscript

The weakness of the foregoing analysis is that it fails to recognise that *the AD and AS curves are not independent*, and that a rising price level will gather momentum should wage increases exceed the rate of inflation. Moreover supply-side measures must not obscure the desirability of working for an agreement on wage moderation.

32 Inflation: Its Effects

32.1 Why Control Inflation?

Definition: Inflation is a sustained rise in money prices generally.

Possible Benefits

1. Slight inflation may *stimulate investment*, but see Internal Disadvantages (3) below.
2. Reduces the real burden of the National Debt through *'fiscal drag'*.

But the rate of inflation tends to *accelerate*.

Internal Disadvantages

1. *Redistributes income arbitrarily*, with the weaker and poorer groups (e.g. retired persons) losing, and stronger groups and debtors gaining; this *undermines stability* between lending and borrowing.
2. *Arbitrary redistribution* may conflict with government policy on redistribution.
3. *Interest rates rise* through (*a*) lenders requiring more, (*b*) government anti-inflation policy. Adverse effect on investment and mortgage repayments.

4. *Discourages saving*.
5. *Encourages borrowing* to buy speculative paper assets having an inflation hedge rather than for real investment.
6. *Distorts resources* into projects having an *inflation hedge*.
7. *Reduces efficiency*: blunting competition as rising prices protect sub-marginal firms; increasing uncertainty; market signals blurred by 'inflation hedge' contracts; disruptions through wage disputes; growth in inflation services simply to advise savers on inflation protection.
8. Frequent *wage renegotiation* generates industrial strife and social unrest.
9. Adds to *administrative costs*, e.g. in revising price lists.
10. Inflation rate gathers *momentum*.
11. Frequent checks to *minimise money balances* waste time.

External Effects

Balance-of-payments deficits occur because:

1. *Exports* drop off.
2. *Imports* increase as home-produced goods become less competitive.
3. *Higher money incomes* increase the demand for imports and divert possible exports to the 'soft' home market.
4. *Liquid capital migrates* to hard currency countries to avoid possible fall in exchange rate.

32.2 A Note on Measuring Changes in the General Level of Prices

There are many different kinds of prices, but usually attention is focused on the prices of goods bought by most people.

Method

Relative changes in prices over time are measured by index numbers. This involves: (*a*) choosing a *base year*; (*b*) selecting a *basket* of a 'typical' family; (*c*) *valuing the basket* at base-year prices, and expressed as 100; (*d*) re-valuing *the basket* at current prices; (*e*) expressing the basket as a *percentage of the base year*.

The usual method is to 'weight' relative price changes of the goods according to relative expenditure on them.

Difficulties

1. Both the basket and the weighting are chosen *arbitrarily* for *particular groups*.
2. The *basket changes* with time.
3. *Technical difficulties* occur in obtaining a *normal base year* and in *collecting information*.

Thus the *Retail Prices Index* is merely an *indicator* of changes in the cost of living. The '*headline*' figure includes mortgage interest payments; the '*underlying*' rate does not.

33 Policies to Achieve Price Stability

33.1 Causes of Inflation: a Simplified Statement

Prices rise when there is an excess of purchasing power for goods available at current prices. Excess purchasing power can arise through:

1. *Demand-pull*. At low levels of employment, an increase in AD is offset by an increase in goods produced. Prices only begin to rise towards full employment as bottlenecks prevent output keeping pace with increases in AD.

   If AD continues to expand after full employment has been reached, we have true inflation.

2. *Cost-push*. The price rise can start on the supply side through import price rises or wage increases which eventually exceed the rate of inflation.

The Phillips Curve

This showed that, over the past 100 years, there was a statistical negative relationship between the annual rate of inflation and the rate of unemployment (Fig. 33.1.). *Policy conclusions*. (*a*) For *demand-pull* inflation, a reduced

**FIGURE 33.1
The Phillips Curve**

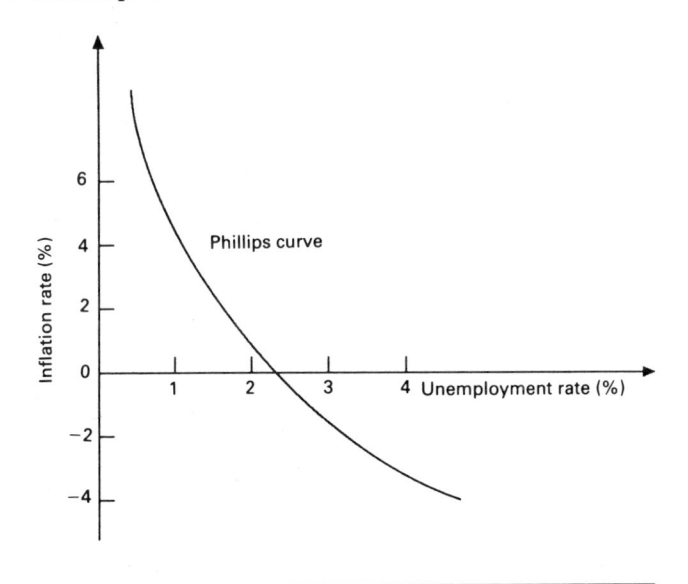

rate of inflation could be 'traded off' against an increase in the rate of unemployment by decreasing *AD*, and vice versa. (*b*) For *cost-push* inflation, the government could seek wage restraint and price control.

Stagflation

In 1960s unemployment and inflation increased together, emphasing that inflation is not a static condition but a *dynamic process* since it enters *expectations*. In other words, the *AD and AS curves are not independent* of each other. In Fig. 33.2 an increase in *AD* to AD_1 produces a rise in the price level. Consequently an increased wage-

FIGURE 33.2
Demand-pull Inflation

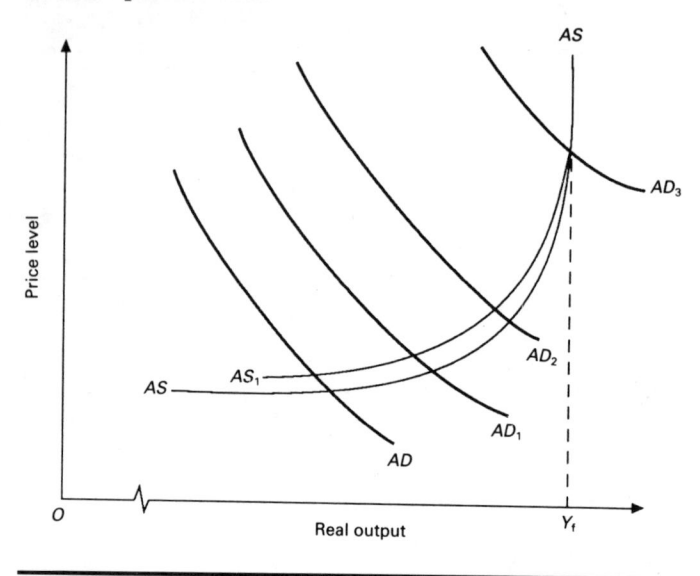

[Figure: Price level vs Real output graph showing AS and AS₁ curves, with AD, AD₁, AD₂, AD₃ curves shifting rightward, intersecting at Y_f]

rate is negotiated, so that the AS curve moves to AS_1. But since this also represents an increase in money spending power, AD moves from AD_1 to AD_2 at a higher price level. This, by generating further wage catching up, produces an inflationary spiral, with the rate of the increase in prices rising, especially when wage rises become geared to an expected higher rate of inflation.

33.2 Monetarism

The monetarist theory of inflation emphasises: (*a*) the *direct impact* of the money supply on AD; (*b*) *expectations* as the cause of the inflationary spiral; and (*c*) the natural *'rate of unemployment'*, as follows.

The Money Supply and AD

The Quantity Theory of Money holds that the general level or prices varies positively and proportionately with the supply of money. It is usually stated in the *Fisher Equation*:

$$P = \frac{MV}{T}$$

where M is the supply of money, V the velocity or circulation, and T the volume of transactions.

But the Fisher Equation is a tautology and is only a *theory* if T and V can be assumed to be constant. Keynes held that, at less than full employment, T would increase, while V would adjust by extra money being held in 'idle' balances.

The *monetarists* (such as Milton Friedman) reject Keynes's view considering that T is fairly constant in the short term and that V has a degree of stability. The latter arises because an increase in M means that cash balances now exceed the fraction of income normally required. Hence the surplus cash is *spent*, not only on bonds, but also *on consumer goods*, leading to a rise in prices.

Inflationary Expectations

Inflationary expectations undermine any trade-off between inflation and unemployment. We have shown (p. 127) that increasing AD may initially reduce unemployment, but eventually trade unions, basing their demands on past inflation experience, negotiate a higher wage rate ('*adaptive expectations*'). If, however, trade unions, applying all available information, can predict the future rate of inflation ('*rational expectations*'), there will be no short-run decrease in unemployment, and the price level rises immediately. Given no change in the real wage-rate, unemployment always reverts to the '*natural rate*'.

33.3 Policy Implications of Monetarist Theory

The government should:

1. *control the money supply* in spite of the difficulty of finding a reliable indicator of M;
2. *influence trade union's expectations* of a lower future rate of inflation by announcing fiscal targets for the medium term and convincing trade unions that these will be adhered to;
3. press ahead with *supply-side measures*.

33.4 Concluding Observations

Reducing AD and urging wage restraint have proved *too simplistic* because:

1. Inflation is a *process*.
2. *Wage rises* are *demanded* irrespective of increasing unemployment or the current level of price rises.
3. Inflation may be closely associated with the *effect of the money supply on AD*.

But since there is no *single* cause of inflation, measures vary and include;

1. Exhortation.
2. Wage restraint.
3. Fiscal policy.
4. Monetary policy.
5. Rigid control of the money supply (see Chap. 43).

34 Economic Growth

34.1 The Nature of Growth

Growth means that *the potential full employment output of the economy is increasing over time*. An annual growth rate of 3 per cent is achievable.

Economic growth can be measured by *increases in real GNP per head* of the population. But *qualifications* may be necessary if: (*a*) the *standard of living* is the main consideration; (*b*) growth is being measured from a *less than full employment* output. Small differences in the annual rate of growth produce large differences in the speed of growth. Growth makes it easier for the government to achieve its economic objectives.

34.2 Achieving Growth

The main causes of growth are:

1. A *rise in the productivity of existing factors* through better organisation and education.
2. An *increase in the stock of factors* through a rise in labour input, the development of natural resources and additions to capital equipment, by '*widening*' capital (maintaining the capital–labour ratio) and by '*deepening*' capital (increasing the capital–labour ratio).

3. *Technological change* – improved capital – promoted by high wage rates relative to the cost of capital.
4. Fundamental changes in the *composition of the national output*, e.g. growth is easier in manufacturing than in services.
5. A sustained improvement in the *terms of trade*.

There are, however, *restraints on growth*, such as: (*a*) failure to *restrict current consumption* by saving: (*b*) *government measures* to combat inflation; (*c*) *balance of payments* difficulties; (*d*) *unemployment* resulting from necessity of *frequent change*; (*e*) *environmental costs*.

34.3 The Government and Growth

The government faces *difficulties*: (a) in *measuring growth*, e.g. the starting point, weaknesses of GNP shortcomings as an indication of the standard of living; (b) in discovering *which factor promotes* most growth; (c) *fluctuations* in the rate of growth are unavoidable, but if considerable may discourage investment.

Government policy must ensure:

1. sufficient real *saving*, e.g. by its taxation policy;
2. adequate *public investment* in the infrastructure, education, etc;
3. that private investment is not '*crowded out*' by public investment or inhibited by '*stop–go*' policies;
4. adequate research and development ($R \& D$);
5. that new *techniques are applied* to produce goods.

35 Balanced Regional Development

35.1 The Regional Problem

AD may be adequate to achieve full employment, but it may not be distributed where idle resources exist. This results from: (*a*) dynamic changes in demand, e.g. jet planes are preferred to ships, and in supply, e.g. natural gas replaces coal in heating; (*b*) frictions preventing adequate response of price system.

Causes of a Regional Problem

1. *Poor natural resources*, resulting in relatively low income, e.g. Highlands of Scotland.
2. *Decline in basic industry*, resulting in a falling level of income and rising unemployment, e.g. South Wales coal.

The classical theory of the correction of the imbalance is through the *price system*, which moves (*a*) workers from low-wage to high-wage occupations, areas and industries, and (*b*) industries from high-wage to low-wage areas. In practice the *market fails* because:

1. The *labour market is imperfect* because of labour immobility, resistance to wage cuts, *national* wage bargaining and inadequate knowledge;
2. increasing returns in manufacturing may attract *capital* to high-wage regions;
3. *external costs* are not allowed for, e.g. lost social capital, disintegration of communities, cumulative depression through multiplier, congestion and inflationary pressure in buoyant regions;
4. *full employment* is assumed.

Consequences of Regional Depression

1. *Under-utilised resources*, with unemployment, social inequity.
2. *Accelerated depreciation* of infrastructure.
3. *External costs* (see above).
4. *Inflation transmitted* from 'over-heated' regions.
5. *EC economic integration*, undermined by possible opposition of 'regional' pressure groups.

35.2 Government Policy

Policy seeks to remedy the above defects, but there may be *incompatibilities*; e.g. sub-optimal location may hamper growth. In broad terms, policy covers: *first aid* through government contracts and the *long-term* 'workers to the work' and 'work to the workers'.

Workers to the Work

This is largely a policy of improving labour mobility. But:

1. Unemployment through immobility is easier to cure if there is *no cyclical* unemployment.

2. *Government interference* with the price system may add to the problem, e.g. rent control.
3. Usually only a *small percentage* of workers have to move from depressed areas.
4. Many changes in occupations and areas can occur through '*ripples*'.

Occupational mobility can be facilitated by: (*a*) providing *information* on opportunities, relaxing trade union entry requirements; (*b*) *re-training*, advice to school-leavers.

Geographical mobility can be improved through the Employment Transfer Scheme: (*a*) *information* on job prospects and in other regions; (*b*) *aid* towards fares, temporary boarding moving costs.

Work to the Workers

Advantages of this policy: it provides for the more immobile workers, maintains communities, relieves congestion in expanding regions, avoids loss of social capital and forestalls a negative 'multiplier' effect. However, it has the *disadvantage* of a loss of locational advantages and thus of higher costs to firms. *Measures* to offset these include:

1. *Assisted Area* policy of *Regional Selective Assistance* based on job creation, capital training costs.
2. *Regional Enterprise Grants* in Development Areas and areas covered by EC schemes – for firms with less than 25 employees.
3. *Removal grants*, loans on favourable terms, cheap government factories, help in transferring key workers, and tax advantages.
4. Some compulsion through *planning* powers.
5. Government-sponsored *industrial estates*.
6. *Dispersal* of government departments.

Regional Planning

Great Britain is divided into ten areas. Each has an Economic Planning Board responsible for the development of its economy and infrastructure.

35.3 Inner City Regeneration

Here older industries have decayed, but workers lack occupational or geographical mobility. *Policy*, co-ordinated by the *Urban Development Agency*, covers:

1. *Enterprise zones* where firms have special benefits;
2. *Derelict land grants* to local authorities;
3. *City grants* for inner city *regeneration* and development;
4. *City challenge*: grants to local authorities on competitive merits of scheme.

35.4 Regional Policy in the Context of the EC

EC integration accentuates the regional problem because: (*a*) *physical controls* on location (e.g. planning requirements) are more *difficult* to apply nationally; (*b*) *peripheral areas* are at a disadvantage; (*c*) EC regions have wider and more varied *economic disparities*.

Therefore, (*a*) EC and national regional policies must be *co-ordinated*; (*b*) *EC's Regional Development Fund*, etc. must be extended, especially to the regions disadvantaged by growth elsewhere.

35.5 Appraisal of Regional Policy

After 60 years of regional policy, *disparities* remain. Up to 1984, capital grants were linked to capital expenditure and cost per job created was nearly £40 000. Also emphasis was on *manufacturing* industry.

In 1984 grants were extended to more labour-intensive *service* industries, and the criterion for grant was switched to *job creation*. But it should be noted that: (*a*) *inefficient labour-intensive* industries may be uncompetitive in the long term; (*b*) firms with modern capital equipment can *compete in export* markets; (*c*) *capital-intensive industries* do *create demand* for *local* labour-intensive *services*.

Conclusion: disparities have not widened. Membership of EC has encouraged *Japanese* and *US firms* to site production *in Assisted Areas*.

36 Public Finance

36.1 The Distribution of Income

Public finance is concerned with *government spending and revenue*, the difference between them (*the PSBR*) and their *magnitude* relative to GDP. We concentrate on the economic characteristics of different taxes especially as regards the government's objectives.

Since welfare cannot be measured objectively, pronouncements on the *distribution* cannot be scientific. But government financial operations do redistribute wealth and the economist can draw attention to the economic implications. The government is concerned with the *distribution of income* for reasons of fairness, social harmony and the effect on the macro variables (e.g. saving). Overall inequality in the distribution of income can be depicted by a *Lorenz curve*.

36.2 Government Expenditure

In 1993, government expenditure is 40 per cent of GDP, and increasing, largely because much is contractual, as with unemployment benefits. It is mainly on: (*a*) defence; (*b*) internal security; (*c*) social responsibilities; (*d*) economic policy; (*e*) miscellaneous items, chiefly interest on the National Debt.

The government has always to *economise*, usually by

making marginal adjustments to its spending on different services. If the government spends more overall, there is less for the private sector, but the relative importance of the two sectors is largely a political decision.

Expenditure is financed by (*a*) borrowing and (*b*) taxation. *Borrowing* is justifiable for large capital projects, and is necessary to cover PSBR. Funds can be raised in the capital market by selling Treasury bills or government longer-term stock, by tapping retail sources, e.g. National Savings, and by privatisation sales.

36.3 The Modern Approach to Taxation

The Attributes of a Good Tax System

Today taxation is not simply revenue-raising but a *macro* instrument of economic and social policy. At the *micro* level, taxes can:

1. *Modify* the influence of *the price system* to: (*a*) protect an *infant industry*; (*b*) develop a *vital industry*; (*c*) help a *depressed industry*; (*d*) compensate for *social costs and social benefits*; (*e*) improve the *terms of trade*; (*f*) improve the *balance of payments*, e.g. taxing imports.
2. Achieve a *greater equality* in the distribution of wealth and income.
3. Secure *other objectives*, e.g. health protection.

This means that Adam Smith's canons of equity, certainty, convenience and economy are now inadequate. A *modern tax system* should be:

1. *Productive* of revenue.
2. *Certain* to the taxpayer.
3. *Convenient*.

4. *Impartial* between similarly-placed persons.
5. *Adjustable*.
6. *Automatic in stabilising* the economy.
7. *Unharmful to effort*. There is little evidence to support the view that a high rate of income tax discourages effort and initiative. Higher marginal rates of tax may do so. Indirect taxes on 'incentive' goods must not price them beyond people's reach.
8. *Consistent* with other policy objectives.
9. Minimal in its effect on the *optimum allocation* of resources.
10. *Equitable*:
    (a) a *regressive* tax takes a smaller proportion of income as income increases;
    (b) a *proportional* tax takes a given proportion of income;
    (c) a *progressive* tax takes a larger proportion of income as income increases. (*If* there is a diminishing marginal utility of income, *progressive taxation* should make for *equity*).

36.4 The Structure of Taxation

No single tax is perfect, so objectives are secured by having a variety of taxes.

1. *Direct taxes*
   (a) *Income tax*: 20 per cent on the first £2500 of taxable income, then 25 per cent, but 40 per cent above £23 700. Allowances are given according to responsibilities.
   (b) *Corporation tax*: 35 per cent under the 'imputation' system, whether distributed or not. Company receives back income tax deducted from shareholders' dividends, which also counts as a tax credit for the shareholder.

(c) *Capital gains tax*: at income tax rate on gains above £5800 in a year on most assets sold, (chiefly securities and property other than one's own house).

(d) *Inheritance tax*: at 40 per cent on legacies and lifetime gifts above £150 000, with exemption for gifts made more than 7 years before death.

(e) *Other taxes*: stamp duties, motor vehicle duties; local Council Tax and Uniform Business Rate.

Direct taxes yield nearly two-thirds of total tax revenue.

2. *Indirect taxes* are collected from sellers who, as far as possible, pass the burden on to the buyers. They may be *specific* (a fixed sum) or *ad valorem* (a percentage of the value of the good). Indirect taxes consist of:

(a) *Customs duties* on goods imported from outside the EC.

(b) *Excise duties* on home-produced goods.

(c) *VAT* – an ad valorem tax levied on the increased value of goods and services at each stage of production. VAT has *advantages*: harmonises with EC indirect taxes; broad-based; does not distort consumers' choice as much as a highly selective tax. But the *disadvantage* is that it tends to be regressive.

36.5 The Advantages and Disadvantages of Direct Taxes

Advantages

1. High and elastic *yield*.
2. *Certainty* as regards payment and yield.
3. *Convenience*.
4. *Automatic* stabilisers of economy.

5. *Equity* by some progression and allowances.
6. More equitable *redistribution of income* and wealth.

Disadvantages

1. *Disincentive* to effort.
2. Can *stifle enterprise*.
3. *Reduce efficiency* incentive.
4. *Reduce funds* for investment at home and from abroad.

36.6 The Advantages and Disadvantages of Indirect Taxes

Advantages

1. *Yield* relieves higher direct taxes.
2. *Certain* and immediate yield.
3. *Convenient* to taxpayer.
4. *Unharmful to effort*.
5. Some *automatic* stabilisation.
6. Further *specific objectives*, e.g. infant industry protection, external benefits and costs policy, balance of payments strengthening.

Disadvantages

1. *Regressive*.
2. *Not completely impartial* through concentration on certain goods.
3. Can *dislocate* industry.
4. *Rigidity*: reduction opposed by protected interests.
5. *Inflationary*, as raise Retail Prices Index.
6. *Distort optimum allocation* of resources, e.g. higher prices affect pattern of consumer spending.

7. Greater *loss of satisfaction* compared with income tax in spending income.

36.7 The Incidence of Taxation

The economist studies the *effective* incidence – how the burden of a tax is eventually distributed.

Direct taxes may adversely affect effort, risk bearing and saving. Moreover, an income tax increase may be passed on in higher wages (and thus prices) by those workers in a strong bargaining position. Taxes on profits will, in the long period, shift production from more risky enterprises, unless the tax falls on monopoly profits.

With *selective taxes* on goods and services, the incidence is split between buyers and sellers according to:

$$\frac{\text{consumers' share of tax}}{\text{producers' share of tax}} = \frac{\text{elasticity of supply}}{\text{elasticity of demand}}$$

Thus: (*a*) a tax on a good where *demand is inelastic* falls mainly on the *consumer*; (*b*) where *supply is inelastic* relative to demand, the tax falls mainly on the *producer*; (*c*) in the long period, consumers tend to bear a higher proportion of the tax; (*d*) if, even in the long period, supply is inelastic, a tax will take longer to pass on to the consumer; (*e*) a *price rise* resulting from a tax will be higher the greater the elasticity of supply relative to elasticity of demand.

With a *subsidy*, the benefit is split between buyers and sellers according to:

$$\frac{\text{consumers' share of subsidy (fall in price paid)}}{\text{producers' share of subsidy (rise in price received)}} = \frac{\text{elasticity of supply}}{\text{elasticity of demand}}$$

Part VIII

International Trade

37 The Nature of International Trade

37.1 Why International Trade?

International trade arises because countries differ in their demand for goods and their ability to produce them. *Factors* of production *cannot be transferred easily* between countries, and so *goods* move instead.

A separate study is made of international trade because: (*a*) *longer distances* are involved; (*b*) problems of *knowledge*, language, currency, etc. present barriers; (*c*) *governments interfere* for economic and political reasons.

37.2 The Advantages of International Trade

1. *Countries can obtain the benefits of specialisation* by concentrating on the production of those goods in which they have the greatest *relative advantage*, provided the *terms of trade* are satisfactory.
2. *Benefits of large-scale production* obtained.
3. *Increases competition*, and efficiency, in production.
4. Promotes *political links*.

37.3 The Terms of Trade (*T of T*)

The Rate of Exchange

For specialisation to take place, the *market* rate of exchange (*t of t*) must be better than the *production possibility* ratios of countries concerned.

Changes in the *t of t* can originate through changes in: (*a*) the conditions of demand and supply; (*b*) currency exchange rates.

Measurement of Changes in the T of T

The *t of t* express the relationship between the price of exports and the price of imports. We measure *relative* changes in the *t of t* between one period and another by *index numbers*. We thus have:

$$\frac{\text{index showing the average price of exports}}{\text{index showing the average price of imports}} \times \frac{100}{1}$$

If exports of *A* become relatively cheaper, the *t of t* have deteriorated, become less favourable or moved against *A*.

Results of Changes in the T of T

1. *Direct benefits of an improvement*:
    (*a*) more imports for given exports;
    (*b*) balance of payments may improve.
2. But *indirect disadvantages*:
    (*a*) countries whose *t of t* have worsened may not be able to *afford* exports of countries whose *t of t* have improved;
    (*b*) *invisible earnings* on foreign investment fall because income and thus spending have fallen in countries whose *t of t* have deteriorated;
    (*c*) with *undeveloped countries*, a fall in income through worse *t of t* may have to be covered by more aid;
    (*d*) changes in the *t of t* may lead to the disadvantages of *frequent fluctuations* in income and employment.

37.4 Free Trade and Protection

Control of International Trade

Only by completely free trade can countries enjoy the maximum advantages of specialisation. Nevertheless, some goods are usually prevented by governments from moving freely by: (*a*) customs duties; (*b*) subsidies; (*c*) quotas; (*d*) exchange control; (*e*) physical controls, e.g. on importing parrots; (*f*) voluntary export restraint. The reasons are:

1. *Non-economic arguments*
    (*a*) to encourage production of strategic goods;
    (*b*) to foster political ties;
    (*c*) to prosecute political objectives;
    (*d*) to promote social policies.

2. *Economic arguments having some justification*
    (*a*) to raise *revenue*, e.g. EC;
    (*b*) to improve *t of t*;
    (*c*) to protect *'infant'* industry;
    (*d*) to enable an industry to *decline* gradually;
    (*e*) to correct a *balance of payments* deficit;
    (*f*) to prevent the *dumping* of goods at a price below that of the home market.

3. *Economic arguments having little validity*
    (*a*) to *retaliate* against other countries' tariffs;
    (*b*) to *maintain home employment* in a depression;
    (*c*) *protect home industries* from 'unfair' foreign competition, e.g. through cheap labour. But:
        (*i*) a country's relative advantage may be cheap labour;
        (*ii*) on this argument, the USA would not import goods from the UK;
        (*iii*) high wage rate countries can still compete through low wage costs per unit;
        (*iv*) increased demand for exports of countries where wage rates are low will raise wages;
        (*v*) trade is better than aid;
        (*vi*) preventing countries from exporting means that they have less to spend on imports;
        (*vii*) protection breeds retaliation;
        (*viii*) protection may enable home firms to raise prices.

General Agreement on Tariffs and Trade (GATT)

This has the object of extending international trade by removing government restrictive measures. Member nations meet periodically to negotiate tariff reductions which must *apply to all countries*. Difficulties:

1. Low-tariff countries begin from an inferior bargaining position as regards concessions.
2. The 'most favoured nation' principle may deter reductions because a country may not wish to apply reduction to all.
3. Special circumstances may necessitate waiving articles of GATT.

The *Uruguay Round* started in 1986, but completion has been delayed by the US view that the EC was 'dumping' her subsidised produce on world markets.

38 The Balance of Payments

38.1 Paying for Imports

Because each country has its own currency: (*a*) sufficient foreign currency has to be obtained to pay for imports; (*b*) a rate has to be established at which one currency will exchange for another. *Imports can be paid* for by:

1. Exports.
2. Invisible earnings through:
    - (*a*) other governments' expenditure;
    - (*b*) sea transport;
    - (*c*) civil aviation;
    - (*d*) travel;
    - (*e*) financial and other services, e.g. royalties;
    - (*f*) interest, profits and dividends from overseas investment;
    - (*g*) private transfers.

38.2 The Balance of Payments

The accounts of a country's transactions with the rest of the world are known as its 'balance of payments'. It is in value terms (£mn).

The Current Account

− imports + exports = *balance of trade* or *visible balance*
− invisible payments + invisible earnings = *invisible balance*

− (deficit) or + (surplus) = *current balance*

The Financial Account

While the current account covers *income* earning and spending, the financial account sets out the currency flow generated by current account balances and *capital movements* in and out of the country. Thus short- and long-term borrowing, realising UK investments abroad and investment by foreigners in the UK add to the UK holding of reserves; and vice versa.

The total currency flow shows how much foreign currency is earned or is required to cover the total of (*a*) the current balance; (*b*) investment and other capital flows; (*c*) the 'balancing item' (the difference between the value of transactions recorded and precise movement of currency known to the B of E). Thus:

+ or − current balance
+ or − investment and other capital flows
+ or − balancing item

+ or − total currency flow

Official financing shows how a net currency outflow was covered, or an inflow allocated. It takes the form of:

− repayments to ⎫
+ drawings from ⎬ IMF and other monetary authorities
− additions to ⎫
+ drawing on ⎬ official reserves

= − or + total currency flow

39 Foreign Exchange Rates

Exchange rates are determined by *demand and supply* of currencies in the foreign exchange market. World-wide arbitrage operations ensure that world exchange rates prevail.

Demand and supply of foreign currencies depend on:

1. Visible trade balance.
2. Invisible trade balance.
3. Movements of capital: (*a*) long-term, (*b*) short-term and (*c*) speculative.

But *underlying economic factors affecting trade and capital movements* are:

1. *Relative prices.*
   Cassel's *Purchasing Power Parity Theory* asserts:

   $$\text{foreign exchange price of £ (in \$)} = \frac{\text{USA price level}}{\text{UK price level}}$$

   But:

   (*a*) all goods do not enter into international trade;
   (*b*) indirect taxes, etc. may cause home prices to rise, but less demand means that less foreign currency is spent, so that the exchange rate improves;

(c) factors other than the price level, e.g. change in income, affect trade flows and thus the exchange rate;

(d) the theory ignores the effect of capital movements on the exchange rate.

Nevertheless, the link between the internal price level and the external value of the currency cannot be ignored because trade and capital flows tend to follow changes in relative price levels.

2. Relative *money incomes*.
3. Long-term *investment prospects*.
4. The *rate of interest*.
5. *Expected future movements* of the exchange rates.
6. *Government expenditure abroad*.
7. *Political factors* and *government policy*.

40 The Correction of a Balance of Payments Disequilibrium

40.1 Alternative Approaches

Where there is a persistent balance of payments (*BOP*) disequilibrium (especially a deficit) corrective measures have to be taken in order to increase earnings from exports and reduce payments for imports.

Basically, exports should be made relatively cheaper and imports relatively dearer by:

1. *reducing expenditure* on imports;
2. *switching expenditure* to increase exports and reduce imports.

40.2 Reducing Expenditure on Imports: Deflation

The Difficulty of Increasing Exports

Because policies to promote exports take time and are only marginal to the problem, the main thrust must be to reduce spending on imports by physical controls and deflation of home incomes.

Physical controls are exercised through:

1. *Imports duties and quotas*. Disadvantages: a loss of comparative cost advantages, protection of home industry may impair efficiency, possible retaliation.
2. *Exchange control* to limit spending on imports and the export of capital. This is essential when the currency is pegged at an over-valued rate, but it has the disadvantages of 'rationing' – inefficiency, evasion, administrative costs, uncertainty in international trade, undermining of financial confidence, purchasing 'second best' goods elsewhere.

Deflation of Home Income

Reducing income leads to a decrease in spending on imports and contains home prices. Its advantage is that the *BOP* is corrected without the obstacle to international trade of uncertain future exchange rates. But: (*a*) home prices, especially wage rates, are inflexible downwards; (*b*) many imports have a low income-elasticity of demand; (*c*) it is really a 'beggar-my-neighbour' policy.

The Gold Standard

The old gold standard was a deflationary mechanism. A country's standard monetary unit was exchangeable for gold at a fixed rate and without restriction. This common link with gold fixed exchange rates between different currencies provided a mechanism for correcting a *BOP* disequilibrium.

Suppose Britain had a *BOP* deficit. Foreign currency would be demanded, but the sterling exchange rate could not fall much as it would soon become cheaper to pay for imports with gold. Results:

1. purchases of gold lowered the banks' cash reserves with the B of E, and thus they had to reduce lending;

2. B of E protected its gold reserves by raising bank rate;
3. higher interest rates attracted foreign capital, halting gold export and discouraging investment;
4. income contraction reduced demand for imports and lowered home prices through a fall in costs. In practice the latter proved difficult, and *unemployment resulted*. Eventually, however, exports did become relatively cheaper.

In the 1930s most countries abandoned the gold standard. It should be noted that maintaining a declared exchange rate under the ERM produced a similar sequence of events.

40.3 Expenditure Switching: Depreciation of the Exchange Rate

The gold standard facilitated trade by maintaining stable exchange rates, but prevented a country following an independent monetary policy to promote full employment. An alternative is to increase export spending and reduce import spending. While the government can control import spending, a more effective method is to lower the exchange rate, which automatically makes exports cheaper and imports relatively dearer.

In a freely operating foreign exchange market, this adjustment is brought about automatically by demand and supply.

Advantages of Exchange Depreciation

1. It avoids the hardship of deflation;
2. Reserves do not have to be protected by administrative controls.

Disadvantages

1. High inelasticity of demand for exports and imports and of supply of exports may worsen the situation.
2. Depreciation of the currency tends to be continuous, especially as the rise in the prices of imports raises home costs and prices;
3. Speculation on future rates accentuates fluctuations;
4. Capital movements affect the exchange rate;
5. Exchange rate fluctuations add to the risks of, and thus reduce, international trade and investment.

40.4 Managed Flexibility

The Exchange Equalisation Account

When the UK left the gold standard in 1931, she had flexible exchange rates, with short-term capital movements being neutralised by the Exchange Equalisation Account buying and selling sterling.

The International Monetary Fund (IMF)

To promote international trade, countries aimed at stabilising exchange rates through the Bretton Woods Agreement, 1944. This established the *International Monetary Fund* (IMF) and the *International Bank for Reconstruction and Development* (IBRD).

'*Managed flexibility*' was operated through the IMF:

1. Each country *declared a value* for its currency in terms of gold, thereby fixing exchange rates;
2. Currencies were *freely convertible* for current transactions;
3. IMF holds reserves of foreign currencies which are

lent to cover a country's short-term *BOP* deficit;
4. Devaluation under agreed rules.

There were two main *weaknesses*: (*a*) exchange depreciation fell mainly on debtor countries (see below); (*b*) international liquidity was not expanded.

Exchange Adjustment

In practice, debtor countries (UK and USA) had to devalue more because creditor countries (Germany and Japan) would not revalue. This imposed periodic deflationary 'stops' on the UK economy as it sought to maintain the existing exchange rate. Any weakness of the pound sterling was magnified by its being a reserve currency. Eventually the pound was floated in 1972, and, with other currencies also floating, the BW system was undermined. Even so countries still carry out limited management of their exchange rate, mainly to offset capital movements.

Successful exchange depreciation/devaluation depends upon the following:

1. the *elasticity of demand* for exports and imports should together be greater than 1;
2. the *supply of exports* should be elastic;
3. the *supply of imports* should be inelastic;
4. *investment income* from abroad should be in terms of the strong currency;
5. other countries should have confidence in a *once-for-all* devaluation.

40.5 International Liquidity

Because the supply of gold did not increase fast enough to finance growing international trade, dollars and sterling were used as 'reserve' currencies instead. But weakness in these currencies made creditors less willing to hold them. Thus Special Drawing Rights (SDRs) were introduced to provide additional liquid reserves. Although the subsequent recession in world trade reduced pressure on international liquidity, SDRs established the principle of internationally created credit.

The International Bank for Reconstruction and Development (the *World Bank*) provides long-term finance at low interest rates for reconstruction and development. Funds are obtained from: (*a*) member nations' subscriptions; (*b*) borrowing on the international market.

Today bridging finance for debtor countries has tended to come from private capital, but the IMF is still important in co-ordinating world-wide economic policy.

41 The European Community

41.1 Background to the EC

After the Second World War, West European nations obtained experience in co-operation through various organisations. But the European Community (EC) goes further, being a *supranational* organisation for integrating the economic policies of member nations. The principle was first applied in 1951 with the European Coal and Steel Community (ECSC). It was extended by the 1957 Treaty of Rome which set up the European Economic Community (EEC) to develop a 'common market' between the six member countries and having its own form of government and institutions. Britain originally remained aloof, forming instead the European Free Trade Area (EFTA). But the success of the EEC and the growth of Western Europe as Britain's main overseas market led to her eventually joining in 1973. The other members are now France, Germany, Italy, Belgium, the Netherlands, Luxembourg, Denmark, the Irish Republic, Greece, Spain and Portugal.

41.2 Institutions of the EC

1. The Commission

This is the most important organ, consisting of seventeen members (including two from Britain) who act in the interests of the Community and not as representatives of individual governments. It makes policy proposals to the Council of Ministers tries to reconcile national viewpoints and executes Council decisions.

2. The Council of Ministers

This contains a Cabinet minister (usually according to the subject under discussion) of each member country. It is the supreme decision-making body, with the task of harmonising the Commission's draft policies with the wishes of member governments. Its decisions are on a weighted majority basis, but unanimity is needed for the politically sensitive areas of taxation, the free movement of people and workers' rights.

The *presidency* of the Council rotates among member states every six months. The outgoing President hosts the *European Council*, a summit of heads of government which seeks to harmonise any differences in views on major strategies.

3. The European Parliament

This is a body of 567 members (87 from UK, directly elected for five years). It debates Community policy, considers its budget and can dismiss the Commission by a two-thirds majority.

4. The Court of Justice

This consists of thirteen judges, one from each country (plus a President). It rules on Community legislation and adjudicates on complaints. Its decisions are binding and have primacy over national law.

5. Special Institutions

These deal with particular policies, e.g. the Economic and Social Committee.

41.3 Economic Objectives of the EC

The aim of the EC – integration and economic policies – is based on:

1. A *Customs Union*, having internal free trade but common external tariffs.
2. A *Common Market (CM)*, where goods and factors of production move freely in response to the price system. This entails '*harmonising*' many aspects of economic policy to produce the *Single Market* in 1993. *Examples* are: a Common External Tariff (CET); a common agricultural policy (CAP); free movement of persons and capital; rules on competition to cover price fixing, market sharing and patents; a common transport policy; indirect taxation harmony; exchange rate stability; common regional and social policies; a Community budget.

41.4 Advantages for the UK of Belonging to the EC

1. Increased possibility of *specialisation* in a 340 mn. market.
2. Increased *efficiency* through competition in the larger market.

3. Faster rate of *growth* through 1 and 2.
4. *Political and defence unity* affording strength in international affairs.
5. *Investment by countries outside* the EC, e.g. Japan and USA.
6. *Assistance to poorer regions* of UK.

41.5 Problems Facing the UK as a Member of the EC

1. The *CET* could lead to trade being diverted towards less efficient EC producers, e.g. of butter.
2. *CAP has disadvantages* for the UK: (*a*) foodstuffs may have to be imported from dearer CM sources; (*b*) high prices encourage over-production; (*c*) the proportionate cost is higher compared with countries where agriculture is more important.
3. '*Dumping*' surplus produce on world markets injures the less developed countries and offends the USA, Australia, etc.
4. An *increasing Community budget*, largely to cover agricultural support, which takes 70 per cent.
5. *Loss of economic sovereignty*, through the ERM, the common monetary policy, VAT rules, the CAP.
6. *Political sovereignty* is surrendered by accepting EC monetary and fiscal requirements.

41.6 The Single Market: 1993

To promote free trade between members, non-tariff barriers have to be removed by harmonisation standards. These were mostly implemented by 1992, enabling the full advantages of a 'common market' to be achievable from 1 January 1993. At present over 50 per cent of the UK's international trade is with the EC.

Part IX

Looking Into the Future

42 The Population of the UK

The population of a country comprises 'households', who are both its consumers and potential labour force.

42.1 The Growth of Population

In 1991, Great Britain's population was just over 56 million. But the rate of growth has fallen from 13 per cent per decade in the nineteenth century to less than 5 per cent in the twentieth.

The rapid nineteenth-century rate of growth was the result of the fall in the death rate combined with a high birth rate. The fall in the twentieth-century rate of growth is due to a fall in the birth rate through a drop in the average size of family, largely through parents' desire for higher children's welfare, social example, competing alternatives and married women continuing to work. Migration has been relatively non-influential.

In 1991, the average family size was 2.2 children and so the population will increase to only about 57.5 mn. by the end of the century. Is this desirable?

42.2 Implications of Changes in the Size of the Population

Theories of Population Growth's Effect on the Standard of Living

Thomas Malthus (1798) held that eventually population would outrun the means of subsistence, and would only be kept in check by famine, disease or war, or by birth control. As regards the UK, however, Malthus's prediction has not been fulfilled, largely because of the fall in the size of the family and the increase in food supplies through imports and improved techniques. Nevertheless, a Malthusian situation exists in the Far East.

Edwin Cannan showed that population could be too small to obtain the full advantages of large-scale production. Thus there must be an '*optimum population*' where, given existing technical knowledge, capital and exchange possibilities, *output per head is at a maximum*. But: (*a*) changes in population affect techniques, etc; (*b*) changing techniques alter the 'optimum'. Thus the concept is of little practical value.

Population Growth and the UK

The UK's population is likely to increase 3 per cent by the end of the century. Is this a good thing?

The *advantage* to the UK of an *increasing population* is that it *stimulates growth* by: (*a*) increasing the *home market*; (*b*) facilitating labour *mobility*; (*c*) stimulating *investment*; (*d*) promoting *vitality*.

The *disadvantages* are: (*a*) resources have to be used to produce *extra capital* rather than consumer goods; (*b*) an increased pressure on the fixed supply of land means that an ever-increasing quantity of *exports* (themselves having an import content) are needed to pay for a given addition to food imports; (*c*) *environmental problems* intensify.

42.3 Age Distribution of the Population

Until the end of the century the UK is likely to have an *ageing population*. This has economic, social and political implications.

1. *Economic*
    (*a*) An *increased dependence* of retired persons on the working population.
    (*b*) A changing pattern of *consumption*.
    (*c*) *Increased health service expenditure*, especially for older persons' needs.
    (*d*) *Less mobility* of labour.
    (*e*) The community may become *less progressive*.
2. *Social*: More home-care services, old people's homes and advice centres required.
3. *Political*: An ageing population *influences government decisions* on immigration, defence weapons, TV and radio programmes, risky investment projects.

42.4 The Industrial Distribution of the Working Population

The *working population*, which equals just under half of Britain's total population is defined *as persons over school-leaving age who work for pay or gain or are claiming unemployment benefit.* It depends on the numbers in the 16–65 age group, its activity rate, the 65+ activity rate, and employment opportunites.

Since 1975, the *working population has increased* by 2.5 mn (10 per cent) of whom 2 mn. are female workers. *Self-employment* has increased by 1.3 mn., largely through governmental encouragement.

Changes in the *industrial distribution* of workers have occurred, chiefly:

1. a 33 per cent *decrease in the primary industries*;
2. a 42 per cent *increase in services*;
3. a 36 per cent *decrease in manufacturing*;

The basic *causes* are:

1. *low income-elasticity of demand* for agricultural products, but high for services;
2. *manufacturing* has *failed to compete internationally* in technical efficiency and wage costs, while North Sea oil exports produced a £ *sterling appreciation*, 1979–84;
3. while *services* are *labour-intensive*, other industries tend to substitute capital for labour.

42.5 The Geographical Distribution of the Population

There are two main features:

1. It is *concentrated*: because industry still centres on coalfield areas and the Midlands and South-East England.
2. It is *urban*: 80 per cent live in towns, with 30 per cent in the seven conurbations, each of over one million people. Within the urban areas, there is a movement from the centre to the suburbs.

Over the past thirty years there has been some movement back to rural areas.

While the *concentration of population* in urban areas allows *more specialised services*, better inter-city transport and greater employment opportunities, it has the *disadvantages* of long-distance travel to work, inner-city decay, less social cohesion and intensified regional unemployment.

43 Current Problems and Policies of the UK

43.1 Introduction

To some extent government stabilisation objectives are *incompatible*; e.g. full employment puts pressure on the price level and the balance of payments. The government, therefore, has frequently to adjust policy to the current situation. Why has the UK been less successful than Germany and Japan in achieving such objectives?

43.2 Inflation

Monetarism, 1979–87

Mrs Thatcher's government in 1979 emphasised the *anti-inflation* objective. Monetarist policy embodied a *medium-term financial strategy* (MTFS) which: (*a*) limited increases in the *money supply*, as measured by M_3; (*b*) *reduced the PSBR* as a percentage of GDP. M_3 proved to be a *misleading measure* as it was not interest-elastic and excluded alternative sources of funds for spending. In 1987, M_0 – an 'indicator', not a 'target' – was substituted and monetary restraint become based on shadowing the sterling–DM exchange rate. *Reducing the PSBR* was necessary because, if covered by short-term borrowing from the banks, it tends to be *inflationary*, while borrowing from the non-bank sector necessitates paying a *higher rate of interest*.

To *support* its *anti-inflation* objective, the government curbed trade union legal powers, limited public sector wage increases and took supply-side measures. The *fall in the rate of inflation* from 18 per cent in 1980 to 4 per cent in 1987 was helped by: (*a*) the *appreciation of sterling* through North Sea oil exports; and (*b*) a relative *high rate of interest* of 13.5 per cent which led to 3.25 mn. unemployed in 1986, thereby curbing demands for wage increases.

Recession, 1989–93

By 1988 the rate of interest had been reduced to 7.5 per cent, the PSBR showed a surplus of revenue over expenditure and 'Big Bang' had freed financial markets. But easier monetary and fiscal policy in response to the temporary stock market crash of October 1987 proved a *blunder*. Imprudent bank lending financed a property boom, and a fall in the personal saving–income ratio from 12.2 to 4.4 per cent fuelled a rapid rise in house prices and an *increase in the inflation rate* to nearly 8 per cent by 1989. Consequently the rate of interest was increased, rising to 15 per cent in October 1989.

The high cost of borrowing led to a *cumulative recession* through reduced investment, increased unemployment, a slump in the demand for houses, a rise in the personal saving ratio, the failure of over-geared property companies and bank write-offs. But *by joining the ERM* in October 1990, the UK had to retain a *high rate of interest* to support an over-valued £1 = 2.95 DM exchange rate. Thus neither a consumer-led nor an export-led recovery materialised, especially as *recession* spread *world-wide*. Only her *suspension of ERM membership* in September 1992 enabled the UK to reduce interest rates.

43.3 The UK's Relationship with the EC

The *Single Market* became operative in January 1993. But M. Delors, the President of the Commission, envisaged complete *monetary union*, including a single currency (the *Maastricht Treaty* 1991). By eliminating exchange rates between EC currencies, there would be a true Single Market, but the single currency and the social chapter were unacceptable to the UK, since they entailed an undermining of her economic and parliamentary sovereignty (a view later taken by Denmark). Her emphasis on '*subsidiarity*' – that powers should be exercised at the lowest possible level – also gained ground.

43.4 Balance of Payments Difficulties

Throughout the twentieth century, the UK has been losing her share of world trade and overseas investment income. Eventually, in 1972, the pound sterling was 'floated'. The sale of *North Sea oil* from 1979 enabled the UK to rebuild overseas investments, but the high £1 = \$2.50 *exchange rate* made her *manufacturing industry uncompetitive* in world markets, forcing a cut in capacity. With dwindling oil exports, the UK has a chronic *balance of payments deficit* of over £12mn. (1992) and this in spite of deflation through the recession, the '*stop–go*' method of correcting a deficit.

Depreciation of the pound sterling followed the UK's

leaving the ERM, but continued depreciation is not a viable policy, chiefly because import prices add to *inflationary pressure*.

43.5 Unemployment

UK unemployment has increased from 1.8mn. in 1989 to nearly 3mn. (1993). Because of the serious balance of payments deficit, a consumer-led recovery must be quickly followed by export-led growth. This requires: (*a*) improved export competitiveness; (*b*) a restructuring of industry.

Lower Wage Costs

Improved competitiveness would come from lower relative wage costs per unit of output. The outlook is promising. Industry has eliminated *surplus capacity*, and *improved labour relations* have diminished trade union power and enabled firms to concentrate on long-term production strategy rather than on settling disputes. A consistent government economic policy which checks inflation and holds down interest rates should encourage *investment* in new products and processes.

These factors should also lead to more *foreign investment* in the UK, especially as firms (Japanese, for instance) seek to establish production bases within the EC. Indeed their improved management and *production techniques could 'spin-off'* onto established domestic firms.

British production must be restructured towards *manufacturing industries*, for these have a tradeable export content of 100 per cent (compared with services' 20 per cent), thereby reversing the decline of the last 20 years as *importers have penetrated the home market*. In particular, the UK should concentrate on developing and exporting new products having a *high income-elasticity of demand*. In addition UK firms must endeavour to regain the *domestic market*.

43.6 Recent Developments

Suspending her membership of the ERM on 16 September 1992 enabled the UK's *rate of interest* to be reduced to 6 per cent by March 1993, and exports to be more competitive through the *depreciation* of sterling. But it also created problems of how to 'kick-start' the economy *and* control *inflation*. Selective taxation reliefs and extra spending on the *infrastructure* add to an already high PSBR. An *inflation policy* of maintaining the underlying rate at below 4 per cent – by aiming at a 4 per cent annual rate of increase in M_0, 'monitoring' other indicators and restricting public sector pay increases to 1.5 per cent – is unconvincing.